Country

Country

Wisdom for a Country Life

David Larkin

A David Larkin Book

Houghton Mifflin Company
Boston New York 2000

CIP data is available.
ISBN 0-618-07707-3
Printed in Italy

SFE 10 9 8 7 6 5 4 3 2 1

COUNTRY is a general introduction to growing things, and is not a field guide. It is the responsibility of the reader to use authoritative field guides for positive identification of all of the wild edibles mentioned in this book. The reader should be aware that any plant substance, whether used in food or medicine, externally or internally, may cause an allergic reaction in some people. The author and publisher assume no responsibility for any adverse effect that an individual may encounter in the use of such substances.

Nature's insecticide. A ladybug will consume fifty aphids a day.

Contents

Introduction

At one moment, in a village store, I picked up the scent of what has since meant the country to me. I was about three years old, and as I held the hand of a grownup, the smells of apples in bins, sides of bacon, roasted coffee beans in sacks, and wood—perhaps from the sawdust on the plank floor—clung together to make one ambiance. I barely knew what I was smelling then, but over the years, in rural America, France, or Britain, where there are

still places that continue to combine these ingredients under one roof, the recognition is a true pleasure.

It surprises me that a dim interior is my first country memory, especially as I was an evacuee. I was part of a whole army of children and mothers suddenly uprooted from the industrial Dockland area of east London, expected to be a target of German bombs when war was declared in late summer of 1939.

We had been sent out into the English countryside, and it was very strange. Of course, all my senses were working, and the sheer greenness of it all from my low perspective was wonderful and I was happy, although not sure why my father wasn't with us. Months later, when he did turn up on leave from the army, I was able to tell him the latest of the country wisdom I had learned: what we had here, and not in the smoky East End, was a thing called *spring* — an occasion when all the trees and the ground were covered in blossoms and lots of baby animals and fluffy chicks arrived.

As far as I was concerned the war could go on forever, but I could detect, as young children usually can, that it was hard on the mothers. The British country people, when duty called, had opened their homes, with good grace for the most part. But the forced separation of families, and hosts with different habits, dialects, and standards meant that the situation could not go on for long. So when the attacks did not come often, and with mistaken optimism that the new shelters and defenses would see us through, we trooped back to London. We arrived home just in time for another adventure following the first Battle of Britain—the Blitz. When the air raid sirens started, usually at night, my sister and I were bundled up in the bedclothes and stuffed into the shelter—something like a New England root cellar—that had been dug in our tiny backyard, and most others too. There, fairly snug, and with the smell of earth around us, we listened to the bombs fall feeling absolutely safe. Following the raids there were sites where bombs had done the most awful destruction, but I saw it all as an adventure playground, a new landscape to which nature and my country experiences could return. There is a story that when Noel Coward, the famous playwright and elegant lyricist, was being driven through the devastation, he saw clumps of white flowers—a form of saxifrage—growing through it all. He asked what the flowers were called, and was told that the local name for this cheery weed was "London Pride." He saw this stubborn seed that just waited for disturbed ground to grow as a symbol of the resilience of the people and their ability to survive, and wrote the moving song of the same name. To me, that plant meant an opportunity to see the occasional browsing bee and white butterfly; but better still, the country came into the city in other ways. In the odd, enclosed patches of spare ground and soccer pitches in the Dockland area, wheat was planted and to our little gang it was Kansas, and went on forever. After squeezing through the railings, we made jungle trails and dens. And, amazingly, this wheat brought with it red poppies, red admiral and tortoiseshell butterflies, even a skylark and other songbirds, and rabbits. I remember pounding a handful of wheat kernels with shrapnel on old brick, trying to make flour.

After the war, the country retreated as the cities struggled to rebuild. It was not a happy time. We had to use our initiative to find the country by bus, even if it was to dig potatoes illegally during the mini-famine of 1947. The Boy Scouts were the answer. A farming family in Essex, whom I know to this day, were most kind to our troop of runny-nosed urchins, letting some of us help with the farm work. I think it was then that the countryside recruited me and my strong visual memory came into play. I soon learned which woods burn well on the campfire, that wood ash is the best cleaner for greasy dixies (pots), that stories around the campfire have an ancient potency. If I was lucky, I could get up extra early to help with the milking. I remember once that my enthusiasm was so great that I spent the night in the cowshed bedded down on fresh straw right next to Wendy, an agreeable Jersey, who lent her body heat to me.

I began to hear rhymes about the weather and to find out which wayside plants were useful, like the dock leaf that soothed the stings of the nettles we collected for soup. There were sayings and odd advice, too, which always seemed to have a connection to the truth, with some straight-faced leg-pulling thrown in. I remember the dairyman telling me that I could get rid of the few summer freckles that marched across my nose and cheeks by the application of fresh cow dung. What he didn't know was that I actually liked this seasonal decoration because a couple of girls in school said they looked cute. What we were both sure of, however, was that I half-believed his cure would work.

In the years that followed, even as a young lad in the city, I kept adding to my country wisdom in various ways: I helped my granddad with his vegetables in the back garden, cutting back invasive mint and covering tomatoes and cucumbers, and as I cycled through the English and French countryside on holidays, I began to identify trees, wild herbs, and mushrooms. I also gathered, here and there, more sayings about the weather and nature, and I became acquainted with the writings of Thomas Tusser, the wise 16th-century Essex farmer. When I finally bought a house and several acres in the country, I began to absorb special knowledge about houses, furniture, outbuildings, wells, wood, and so on, while adding to my knowledge of trees, wild plants, weather, lore, and gardening.

Here is my collected country wisdom for all of you who have left the city to work at home as our society restructures itself, for all of you who already have a weekend house or just like exploring the countryside, and for all of you who dream and plan for a house in the country.

From "London Pride"
by Noel Coward

There's a little city flow'r-
ev'ry spring unfailing
Growing in the crevices
by some London railing
Tho' it has a Latin name,
in town and countryside
We in England
call it London Pride.

London Pride has been
handed down to us.
London Pride is a flower
that's free.
London Pride means
our own dear town to us,
And our pride
it for ever will be.

A Walk on the Wild Side

When I found the time to explore our piece of land after we moved in, I made for the edges of the fields, the overgrown stone walls, the paths, and old logging trails where the action takes place. There are more varieties of plants, flowers, trees, fungi, insects, birds, and animals to be found here than in the deep woods and wide open fields.

The first summer after our fields stopped being grazed or mowed years ago, here's what happened: By midsummer, the new arrivals, mostly borne by the wind and birds, were annual plants — dandelion, chickweed, and ragweed. The next summer the ragweed poisoned its own patch of ground and itself, dying off after its seeds were blown to another spot. Following came some biennials — Queen-Anne's-lace, mullein, and burdock — stronger plants pollinated by insects. And last, perennials — goldenrod, aster, joe-pye weed, black-eyed Susan, and maybe the first tiny blackberry and strawberry shoots. This thicker cover, along with insects and seeds, attracted more birds and small rodents, followed by their predators. The first trees moved out from the shady field edges: clusters of spindly white birch, aspen, poplar, and here and there an occasional white pine. These are short-lived for trees, grow quickly and have created cover for the slow-growing oak, ash, beech, and maples that eventually take over. These latter easily outlive humans by a hundred years or so, and die slowly. Underneath, the original pioneer plants would be long gone, but seeds will remain in the ground, waiting for the next cycle of opportunity.

Soon after the land was first cultivated, native plants had to compete with alien invaders. The resident species had numbers in their favor, with generations of dormant

seeds waiting in the ground. But the weeds brought by the colonists were aggressive (a quarter of the plants growing in your meadow originated in Europe). Many alien plants, birds, and animals seem to thrive away from the competition they face in their native lands. Imported starlings, for example, have reduced the population of native woodpeckers, bluebirds, and swallows that have the same nesting patterns. By the same token, on the other side of the Atlantic, the American gray squirrel has almost eliminated the native European red species.

I usually leave a twenty-foot area between the cultivated field and the woods. There, brush cutting and mowing preserve the variety of wildflowers. It's as if this area were regularly grazed and browsed by hoofed animals.

Going back to nature sometimes has its ugly moments, even for those of us who see the unmown field as a potential meadow of wildflowers and butterflies floating in the summer haze. Many of the first invaders have a rough, scrubby look about them that would make them seem at home in an abandoned city lot. Nevertheless, the simple picture above contains many valuable plants. In the foreground are burdock and nettle, sources of food. In the middle ground, goldenrod and aster, valued as medicine. Behind them, in front of a wild apple tree, is the uniquely American Jerusalem artichoke — about the only native in this scene. The tubers from this plant are excellent substitutes for potatoes. A dieter's delight, they are low in starch.

Our daily bread, pasta, rice, or oatmeal all come from different forms of grass. It is the greatest single source of nutrition in the world. Grasses are the only plants we cannot do without.

In the Woods

Preceding page. These trees, seen in the spring, have been thinned to demonstrate the variety of species. Shown are, left to right, dogwood, tulip tree, and oak.

When young, the slow-growing beech protects its vulnerable leaf joints by retaining some of its leaves throughout the winter until new shoots appear; it is sealing its vulnerable abscission zone, where the stem of the leaf joins the branch. The leaves are pushed off by new growth in the spring. As the tree gets older and stronger, it sheds its leaves like other deciduous trees.

Late in the fall is the best time to count the oak trees in your woods. They are the last to lose their leaves.

On previously cleared land, pioneer trees come up fast — first birches, conifers, and aspens, then ash. Size is not important in the first thirty years. After that the disparity becomes apparent. Birches, aspens, and cedars die of old age. They gradually give way to harder woods such as oaks and hickories. Even these will not outlast the slower growing beeches and maples. Left alone, most forests will eventually become almost entirely deciduous.

White pines can be seen behind some sugar maples.

White pine, the most important tree of Colonial America, is easy to work with, and by 1900 it had been almost totally depleted. It was used for shipbuilding (white pine grows straight and long-grained, solid yet supple, making it perfect for masts), houses, farm buildings, furniture, and even matchsticks. Trees were then extensively replanted by hand labor and began to regenerate naturally. White pine appears all over my land and is very quick to grow. For example, tiny saplings were planted along our driveway about twenty years ago by the previous owner. Still young, they are already thirty feet tall and will soon screen us completely from the road. The white pine is easily distinguished from other pines by its cluster of five needles joined together.

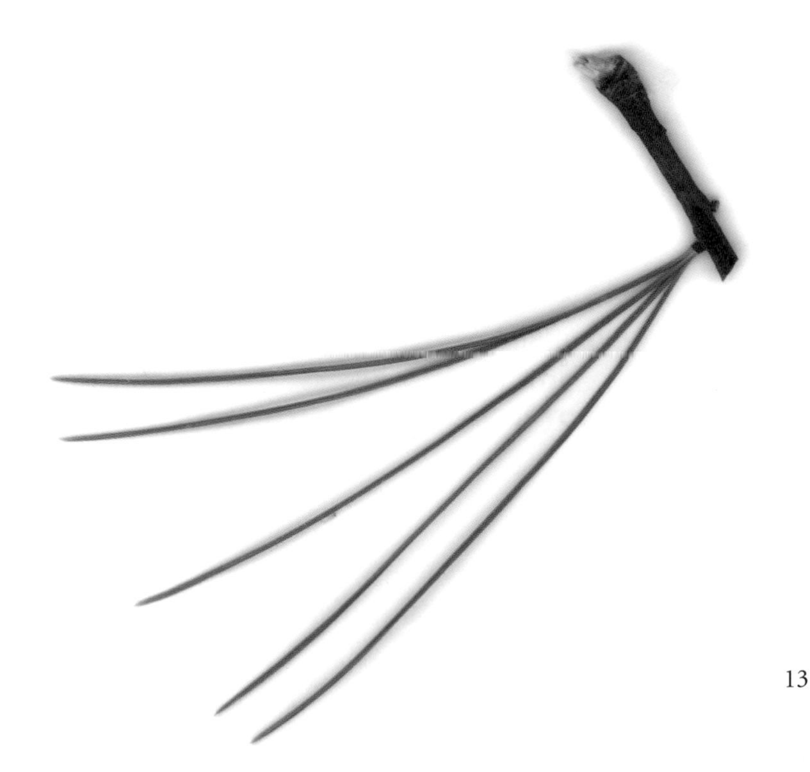

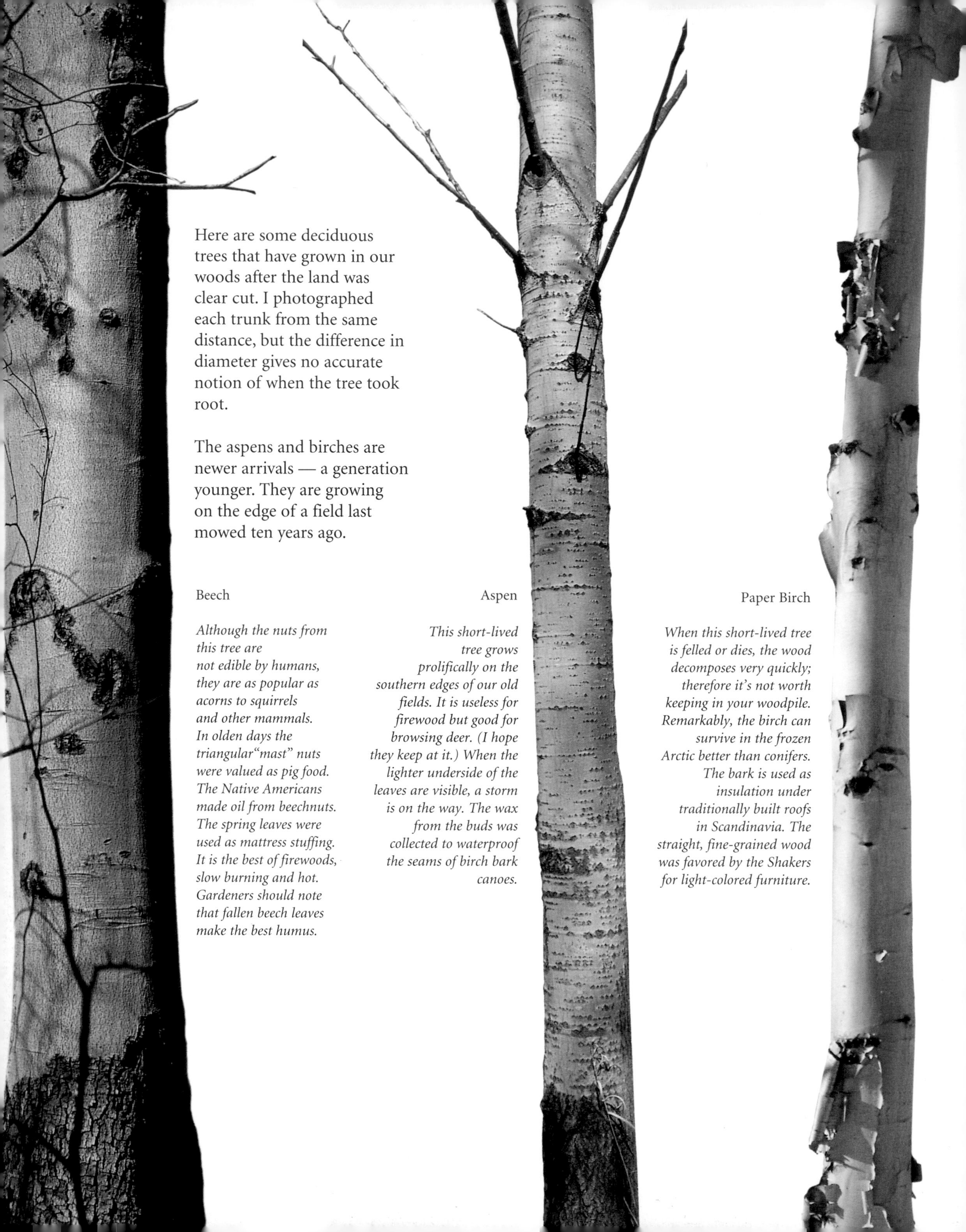

Here are some deciduous trees that have grown in our woods after the land was clear cut. I photographed each trunk from the same distance, but the difference in diameter gives no accurate notion of when the tree took root.

The aspens and birches are newer arrivals — a generation younger. They are growing on the edge of a field last mowed ten years ago.

Beech

Although the nuts from this tree are not edible by humans, they are as popular as acorns to squirrels and other mammals. In olden days the triangular "mast" nuts were valued as pig food. The Native Americans made oil from beechnuts. The spring leaves were used as mattress stuffing. It is the best of firewoods, slow burning and hot. Gardeners should note that fallen beech leaves make the best humus.

Aspen

This short-lived tree grows prolifically on the southern edges of our old fields. It is useless for firewood but good for browsing deer. (I hope they keep at it.) When the lighter underside of the leaves are visible, a storm is on the way. The wax from the buds was collected to waterproof the seams of birch bark canoes.

Paper Birch

When this short-lived tree is felled or dies, the wood decomposes very quickly; therefore it's not worth keeping in your woodpile. Remarkably, the birch can survive in the frozen Arctic better than conifers. The bark is used as insulation under traditionally built roofs in Scandinavia. The straight, fine-grained wood was favored by the Shakers for light-colored furniture.

White Ash

Overcrowding causes all the trunks of our ash trees to grow straight and narrow before their branches form a canopy. Young ash leaves were made into a tea to relieve rheumatism and gout. Prized as a timber tree for its strength and flexibility, it will bend before breaking. It is the stuff of baseball bats.

Sugar Maple

We have more of these hard and useful trees than any other on our land. The timber value of mature maples is higher than most other hardwoods. *See page 147 for instructions in syrup making.*

White Oak

A valuable tree for timber, the strongest of our native woods. Left alone it produces acorns less bitter than those of red and black oaks. *See page 148 for their use.* *Try not to shelter from the rain under this tree, as it is said to attract lightning.*

The uniform green of summer leaves gives way to many shades in the fall. This is the best time to identify the trees around you.

Red Maple

White Oak

Norway Maple

Willow Oak

Shumard's Red Oak

Pin Oak

Scarlet Oak
Sweet Gum
Yellow Buckeye
Tulip Tree
London Plane

Watercourses

Fast-moving streams coursing through high woodlands create slippery, moss-covered rocks. This stream dwindled down in high summer to a series of tinkling waterfalls. When tested at this time of year, the water was less acidic than at other times, since it was now pushing through limestone rocks under the granite and gravel. Rushing streams don't leave sufficient sediment in the water for plants — growth is on the banks where they can take root against the current.

The sediment pushed downstream is full of organic material. As the water seeks the quickest way to a lower level, it alters course to form shoals and oxbows of fine silt, perfect for establishing moisture-loving plants. Every small stream bed is part of a larger watercourse that becomes a habitat for many plants. The edges of a track or road following the stream or river, even some distance inland, will be full of variety. The stream is a corridor of life, and also the road for animals and birds. Lower down in the valley, as the stream becomes a river, willows and alders slow and calm the flow; in cultivated areas they often were planted to stay the river's course and stop erosion of its banks.

Even more fertile are the areas connected to an established lake, pond, or slow-moving stream — these are wetlands and marshes, the richest, most valuable and endangered of all natural places. In the past, wetlands, difficult to develop, were therefore rarely settled. More recently, wetlands have been threatened by sophisticated drainage schemes developed by those who see such terrain as cheap real estate or nutrient-rich farmland.

These moss-covered rocks are a breeding ground for black flies.

Marshlands, bogs, and fens change little in appearance year after year, because decomposition is so slow. They have become the best places for recording an area's natural history. Seeds, pollen, timber, and even human bodies with evidence of their last meal still in their stomachs have remained intact for thousands of years in frozen wetlands.

Arrowhead or Wapato (*Sagittaria latifolia*)

This perennial grows on the edges of lakes, ponds, and swamps throughout most of the United States. It has arrow-shaped leaves that vary greatly in size, and three-petaled, white flowers. A favorite food of the Native Americans, Lewis and Clark and other explorers learned about it in their travels. And when the first Chinese were brought to California as laborers, they quickly adopted this plant to supplement their diet.

The small, round tubers attached to the runners of the actual root are the edible part of the plant. They are best collected in the fall, when the leaves of the arrowhead have turned brown. It's a messy and cold harvest, so boots are recommended as well as a small pitchfork or rake to pull the plants out of the mud. The tubers taste rather like potatoes when boiled, roasted, or fried. They are more easily peeled after cooking than when raw.

Marsh Marigold or Cowslip (*Caltha palustris*)

One of the first flowers of spring is the cowslip, which pops up in swamps, wet meadows, and marshy places. It has flowers with five petal-like sepals of golden yellow, and bright green, heart-shaped leaves. In colonial days it was well-known in New England where the leaves, picked young, were a spring tonic, rich in minerals and vitamins provided by nutrients in the drainage from higher areas.

This plant must *always* be cooked, since in the raw state it contains an acrid poison that must be dispelled by the cooking process. It should be boiled in salted water for several minutes, then drained and boiled again for six to eight minutes and drained once more. It can then be tossed with butter and salt. The other edible part is the unopened flower bud first boiled twice to remove the poison, then pickled and enjoyed as a caper substitute.

Purple loosestrife *(Lythrum Salicaria)* grows in ditches, wet fields, and swampy areas. A European import, it is considered a nuisance because of its invasive tendencies and ability to crowd out native species important to birds and other wildlife. However, it does have a lovely spike of purple-pink flowers atop a tall stem. The whole plant, when dried and used as a tea, was a folk remedy for dysentery. The tea also was used as a gargle, and applied as a disinfectant for wounds.

Swamp-cypress (*Taxodium distichum*) spends most of the year with its cone-shaped "knees," which project from submerged roots, poking out of water. Here it is seen in the dry season. The heartwood was harvested for its resistance to decay. Those cypress swamps still remaining are usually protected areas, serving as important, richly organic transitional zones.

Signs of Animals

Animals in the country — unlike well-behaved children — are usually heard but not seen. Tracks in the mud or snow give us the best indication of their actual whereabouts. In addition, their presence is made known by the sounds they make on spring, summer, and autumn nights, the loudest coming from the combat zone on the edge of the forest. (P.D. James, in one of her novels, has a country-wise old tramp say that he has experienced more violence in a hedgerow than in the meanest parts of a great city.) When we see them on our place, the foxes and coyotes are just passing through, more familiar with the details of their large territory than we could ever be. We also see raccoons, skunks, and opossums at dusk, like anyone in the country who owns a compost heap. Our German shepherd and half-wild barn cat have enough sense to let them be. Our dog, as a pup, learned from experience — her encounter with a porcupine required the vet to pull a quiver full of quills from her muzzle.

Animals take flight from a human face and from a body with arms swinging out from the sides; if you want to observe one at close range, walk slowly, take small steps, and hold your arms in — don't look like a scarecrow. Avoid facing the animal directly, so your face doesn't reflect light.

On the following pages are some of our neighbors, their footprints illustrated closer to the eye than commonly seen, and in better light. However adept some animals are at making themselves disappear, they have not yet learned to cover their tracks.

The **beaver** is busy at night, working as well as eating bark and small twigs. A beaver lodge soon turns into a busy family compound when the four or so kits still in the lodge are joined by the current season's young. A group of ten to twelve all working away together is not unusual, until the lack of raw material forces the newer arrivals to move on. After being close to extermination, the recovering beaver populations are becoming something of a problem in New England and other regions, where free-flowing rivers are blocked and planned reforestation flooded. We see lodges all over our area but rarely see beavers, who are mostly tucked inside until dusk. Beavers can remain underwater for a long time — a beaver can swim for half a mile with one gulp of air.

These **raccoon** tracks, visible in early morning light, were made in wet sand. They will disappear as the sun evaporates the moisture and a breeze begins to blow.

Raccoons occasionally make night raids on our bird feeder, but otherwise seem to have an understanding with our cat and dog. Judging by the way raccoons make off with sweet corn cobs from our compost pile, we are probably wise not to grow corn. Raccoons give country people a lot of pleasure because of their cleverness, but, sadly, we have had to remove two rabid ones from our property. Their common name comes from the Algonquin Indian word *aroughcun* meaning "he scratches with his hands."

Studies of its diet show that the fox does more good for the farmer than harm, consuming more mice, rats, and wild rabbits than it does farmyard ducks and chickens. The red fox was imported from England for the pleasure of fox-hunting landowners. Today's version is a mixture of the red and the native gray fox — which is no fun to chase because it is slow and climbs trees. There are about four million red foxes in the United States, and that number is likely to remain stable because of the competition for food and territory with coyotes, now on the increase. This young fox was photographed just after a pleasurable roll in the morning dew.

We often see a black **mink** moving at great speed along our stream banks. There may be only one, as they are extremely territorial and their hunting range can stretch for several miles along a river or stream.

The **moose** is the largest member of the deer family. These are the light footprints of an animal that can reach a weight of more than 1,400 pounds. Normally, moose are docile and ignore or shy away from humans. However, don't crowd a bull during breeding season (September-October) or a cow with young ones (May-June) — either one will charge and can cause severe injury.

During several studies, biologists observed that deer are likely to be most active on cloudy and moonless nights when they feel more secure in the open and are least visible to predators. They have excellent night vision and don't need moonlight to see and function well. As human population grows, and deer become more familiar with our behavior, their own habits take some strange turns. Deer are very inquisitive. Plant something, and they come round to see what it is. When they hear the noise of human activity they feel safe. A chugging tractor engine stops, and they look up and bolt. When we are around, silence is what scares them.

Moving out of the cover of woods, this stag is in an overgrown field, a favorite spot for browsing. It is also the territory of the tick that carries Lyme disease. *See page 74 on how to protect yourself from this dangerous parasite.*

If you ever come across a baby fawn hiding in the long grass, leave it alone; it has not been abandoned. The mother is waiting nearby until you are well away before it comes back.

Folklore:
In Punxsutawney, Pa., on Groundhog Day, the woodchuck known as Punxsutawney Phil awakens from its long winter sleep and pokes its head out of the ground. If the sun is shining and the groundhog can see its shadow, winter will supposedly last another six weeks; if it's cloudy and the groundhog cannot see its shadow, it means that spring will arrive sooner.

The tradition began when German settlers arrived in Punxsutawney, a town between the Allegheny and Susquehanna rivers, in the early 1800s; they brought with them a tradition called Candlemas Day. In Germany, a badger's reaction to its shadow was watched on February 2. In Pennsylvania, the male groundhog, awakening from hibernation, was deemed a sensible replacement.

Except for the mountain-loving hoary marmot, large ground squirrels, comprising woodchucks (groundhogs) and prairie dogs, are not popular with those engaged in cultivation. Woodchucks are only interested in young, succulent plants and, as gardeners know, they will travel and expend much effort to reach them. But woodchucks do a lot of good in the wild; their burrows are reused or enlarged by other animals, and in New York state alone, it was estimated that they turned over and aerated 1,600,000 tons of soil in one year.

True hibernation is close to death for some mammals. The groundhog gives us the best example of this phenomenon. After frantic feeding in late summer and early fall, the groundhog retires to a sleeping chamber and walls itself in with dirt. Once asleep, the groundhog's metabolism drops to a very low rate: its body temperature, close to our own at 97F when active, decreases to around 60F; heart rate slows to only one beat per minute; and a breath is taken only once every five minutes. Undisturbed, it will stay in this deathlike sleep for more than five months.

The Great Plains can be brutally hot during the summer, but colonies of prairie dogs use special techniques to keep their burrows cool and comfortable. A typical burrow is a two-ended tunnel between fifty and eighty feet long, with the shape of the entrances key to freshening the underground air.

Prairie dogs build one entrance with dirt piled in a cone-shaped mound around the hole, while the other entrance is low and almost flat. When the wind blows, the difference in elevation creates a vacuum that draws air to the higher entrance from the lower.

The system works so well that scientists estimate even a one mph breeze will create a complete air exchange every ten minutes. Even better, the flat prairie allows the system to work no matter in which direction the wind is blowing.

Coyotes have moved slowly back from the West to the East to occupy former wolf territory, picking up some wolf blood on the way and developing into a subspecies, the Eastern coyote. We see them about as frequently as we see black bears, which is not very often. As the territory for each is large, and we can't get very near, we may be looking at the same animals over and over again. Unlike the perpetual-motion fox, coyotes will sit still when caught unaware, but they are just as shy as foxes and will soon move quietly and calmly away. We often hear coyotes at night making their social calls in the next hollow.

This odd-looking trail was made by an **otter** whose heavy tail pressed into the snow, making a trough. The interruptions were made by its paws as the otter periodically gave itself a push, rather like a cross-country skier. Otters can toboggan down slopes skillfully — often returning just for the pleasure of another ride. The otter's body is so streamlined it can dive into the water leaving scarcely a ripple. The otter also can snack on small catches while swimming along on its back, steering with its tail.

Tracks of the eastern coyote

You may or may not ever see the creatures that inhabit the forest, but they are present in higher numbers than you might imagine. For example, based on a survey of 1,000 acres of eastern deciduous forest not far from where I live, an extremely rough estimate of wildlife population follows:

1 billion arthropods (insects, spiders, etc.) large enough to be seen with the naked eye
900 pairs of small nesting birds
25,000 mice
3,500 squirrels
20 white-tailed deer
35 wild turkeys
8 predatory birds (hawks, owls, etc.)
4 foxes
1 bear
1 coyote
plus other assorted animals: woodchucks, raccoons, voles, chipmunks, opossums, skunks, rabbits, etc.

Ranges and Areas

Some animals operate from their dens, or within limited areas; others travel several miles each day in search of food, before returning home. Browsers are always on the move within their own territory.

Opossum—20-30 acres

Black bear—15 miles

Raccoon—2 miles

Skunk—20 acres

Coyote—10 miles

Red fox—2 miles

Gray fox—5 miles

Bobcat, Lynx—25-50 miles

Woodchuck—30-100 acres

Ground squirrel—1 per acre

Chipmunk—2-4 per acre

Gray squirrel—2-10 per acre

Red squirrel—4-8 per acre

Cottontail rabbit—2 per acre

White-tailed deer—1 mile

Moose—2 per square mile

Animal populations have peaks and declines that are quite regular and part of a natural cycle — despite the impact man has on them.

The peak years for rabbits, coyotes, muskrats, caterpillars, and foxes were, and will be, 1981, 1991, and 1999.
Game birds peak approximately every seven years.

Night Eyes

Here are the colors of animals' eyes caught at night by flashlight or headlights.

Deer—bluish white

Wolf, Coyote—greenish/orange

Dog, Fox—pale green/white

Bobcat, Lynx—pale yellow

Raccoon—bright yellow

Opossum—pale orange

Bear—bright orange

Skunk—amber/red

Rabbit—pale violet to white

Jack rabbit—pink

Bullfrog—green

Otter—pale amber

Natural life spans
(*in years*)

Pelican—40-50

Large reptile—25-30

Toad—30

Bear—25-30

Deer—18-25

Domestic cat—17-20

Coyote—12-15

Songbird—10-15

Domestic dog, Wolf—10-15

Beaver—10-12

Otter—10-12

Raccoon—10

Squirrel, Rabbit—10

Fox—8-10

Bat—5

Small rodent—3-5

Shrew—1

The pattern on butterfly wings distracts any predators. To confuse their enemies further, some butterflies taste bad and some edible ones have wing patterns that imitate their unpleasant-tasting kin. I remember that I had to catch white butterflies to save our cabbages (grandfather did not use pesticides), and after picking them off while they folded their wings to lay eggs, I noticed that my fingertips had the highly concentrated stink of rotten cabbage. Defense goes on in the insect world. The light of the firefly would normally be expected to attract predators, but the chemicals that create the insect's glow also make it inedible.

The useful ladybird's bright color advertises that it will taste bad, too.

The Canadian tiger swallowtail

Above: a blue darner dragonfly
Right: a skimmer

While up at our pond fishing and being still, I become part of the life there. One begins to see how a Thoreau could report on so much activity within his sight. The frogs rarely move, the water boatmen skiff only for short distances, and the dragonflies supply most of the movement and sound from whirring wings as they constantly patrol the pond shore, gobbling up the midges that plague me. The midges and mosquitoes have no hope — it seems that while catching one the dragonfly already marks the next. The dragonfly is able to fly in bursts of thirty mph, flying backward, sideways, upside down, and braking suddenly. I see the value of having cattails, reeds, and sedges at the pond edge; they become carrier decks to launch from when the dragonfly takes off after its prey.

Butterflies are more plentiful on sunny days, when flowers release more nectar. The butterflies in our area favor three plants that flower near our house. The yellow Canadian swallowtails come to our chives in great numbers and rarely go anywhere else. Many other species seem to like a very suburban-looking viburnum shrub and, most unlikely, the spotted joe-pye weed (*Eupatorium maculatum*). (It may be truth or it may be legend, but it is said that the common name of this perennial goes back to Colonial times when an Indian named Joe Pye favored it for its healing powers.)

A brushfoot on joe-pye weed

Medicinal and Useful Plants

Common St. Johnswort

(*Hypericum perforatum*)

In Europe, the flowering top parts of this plant have been dried and used for centuries in the form of an infusion, to relieve depression, anxiety, and tension. St. Johnswort is also highly regarded for the healing properties of an infused red oil, made from its flowers and leaves, reported to have been carried by Crusaders in the Middle Ages to heal their wounds. This oil is also applied for the relief of bruises, arthritic joints, skin rashes, and sprains.

Native to Europe, western Asia and North Africa, St. Johnswort is an import to the United States. It is commonly seen growing on dry banks, in fields, and in clearings. The oblong leaves of this one-to-three-foot-tall perennial have numerous translucent glandular dots that look like tiny punctures when held up to the light. The flowers have five golden-yellow petals and bloom from June to August.

There are ancient superstitions relating to St. Johnswort. Its generic name is derived from the Greek *hypericum* meaning "over an apparition," a reference to the belief that the herb was so unpleasant to evil spirits that one whiff would cause them to disappear. Also, on St. John's Eve, June 24, it has traditionally been gathered and hung in windows or on doors to ward off evil spirits.

St. Johnswort can be cultivated in an herb garden. It likes moist soil and partial shade.

Sweet Goldenrod *(Solidago odora)*

In the 18th century, at the time of the American Revolution, this was one of the major herbs substituted for China tea in defiance of the British "tea tax." Tiny yellow flowers, typical of all the goldenrods, are massed in clusters at the top of the stem. Unlike other goldenrods, however, this one has smooth, toothless leaves three or four inches long that release an anise-like fragrance when crushed.

The leaves, fresh or dried, can be steeped in hot water to make a pleasant drink, often referred to as "patriot tea." It also has been administered medicinally for problems of the digestive system. Sweet goldenrod thrives throughout most of the United States, attracting bees and butterflies when in full bloom. Contrary to popular myth, goldenrod pollen is not responsible for allergic sneezing — the real culprit is ragweed.

Wormwood (*Artemisia absinthium*)

The common name of this bitter, aromatic perennial relates to its use as a vermifuge. It also was thought to be useful as a moth repellent for fabrics, and as a flea deterrent strewn on floors. It has been valued for centuries for its medicinal properties incuding the relief of indigestion, fevers, rheumatism, gout and liver problems. However, wormwood is dangerous and poisonous when taken in excess. An extract from the root was the basis of the doubly potent addictive liqueur *absinthe* that reportedly killed Toulouse Lautrec and others until the drink was made illegal. Today, with the toxic ingredient removed, it is used as a flavoring for wines, aperitifs and other drinks, and healing teas are made from dried leaves infused in boiling water.

Common Yarrow (*Achillea Millefolium*)

We planted yarrow in our garden for the beauty of its small flowers and delicate, feathery leaves, even though it can be found growing wild in fields and all along the roads in summer. We knew this aromatic herb had traditionally been made into a medicinal tea, but it took several years before we got around to making some ourselves. The tops of the flowering stems are collected and dried for this use while the flowers are still in their prime. They should be crumbled and stored in glass jars. To make an infusion, or tea, put dried yarrow and boiling water into a teapot in the following proportions: one tablespoon of yarrow to one cup of water. Let it steep for ten minutes, strain, and then drink. The tea will have a pleasant smell and a slightly bitter taste.

Yarrow tea is reputed to be valuable as a general tonic and as an aid to digestion. Primarily anti-spasmodic and anti-inflammatory, it has been recommended as a medicine for colds and fevers, stomach cramps, gynecological problems, blood circulation, and hemorrhaging of the lungs and kidneys.

Giant Hogweed

(*Heracleum Mantegazzianum*)

This invasive and noxious plant comes from the Caucasus mountains of Asia, and was privately cultivated as an exotic during the Victorian period in England and the United States. However, it has now escaped such cultivation and invaded the wild in both countries. The plants can grow up to fifteen feet tall. When the stems are broken they produce large amounts of sap that causes severe irritation, swelling, and painful blistering of the skin that requires medical treatment. The hogweed is a relative of the carrot, producing a large, tuberous root that is difficult to dislodge. The sharp-eyed reader may recognize Joanna Lumley, an enthusiastic countryside defender, contending with a decidedly non-fabulous hogweed on her land.

Queen-Anne's-lace, or wild carrot, is a tiny and distant relative of the giant hogweed.

Growing up to six feet tall, **teasel** (*Dipsacus Sylvestris*) has a prickly, thistlelike head with small, purple flowers. It was brought from Europe to grow commercially for the dried heads, which "teased," or raised, the nap on woolen cloth. Today this biennial is naturalized throughout North America and often used in dried flower arrangements.

Skeins of dyed wool from natural colors. They are, left to right: natural, hickory bark and copperas, osage orange and alum, cochineal, tree lichen and alum, log wood and alum, osage orange and copper sulfate, madder root, osage orange and copperas, osage orange and cream of tartar.

Plants have been used in **dyes** for thousands of years. To prevent the color from fading, a process known as mordanting, or fixing, is necessary to make the color both permanent and richer. Animal or vegetable fibers are usually soaked, boiled, or simmered in the mordanting agent before dyeing takes place. The most common of the agents are aluminum, chrome, copper, tin, and iron in usable form. If this brief introduction captures your interest, there are excellent books available to which you can turn for specific instructions. On this page you'll find examples of colors you can produce from plants, trees, and nuts described in other sections of this book. Of course, there are many other plants good for dye including indigo, famous for its blues.

Natural dyeing of wool from the sheep at Hancock Shaker Village.

Sources of natural dyes

Acorns: bark and acorns give tan

Barberry: roots give yellow and deep green

Sweet Birch: bark offers shades of brown

Blackberry: berries give purple and gray

Bracken: young shoots offer yellowish-green

Chamomile: flowers offer shades of gold

Coltsfoot: leaves give a greenish-yellow

Currants: juice gives shades of lilac to purple

Dandelion: blossoms offer shades of yellow

Daylily: blossoms give yellow, gold, and blue-gray

Elderberry: berries give purple, blue, and blue-gray

Goldenrod: blossoms give shades of lemon yellow to gold

Hickory: hulls and bark give tan

Grapes: ripe grapes give purple

Stinging nettle: whole plant gives greenish-yellow

Beach plum: leaves give yellow

Raspberries: juice gives pink to purple

Sassafras: leaves and bark offer reddish tan, black, and gray

Sumac: berries give yellowish-tan, gray, tan, and brown

Walnut: hulls offer dark brown

Wild Food

Preceding pages: Wild raspberries in blossom

Edible Plants

It's my belief that the more we learn about the value of wild plants, the more we will want to encourage and protect them. Flower and vegetable gardeners may take special delight in eating the weeds that plague them. Many of the plants displayed on the following pages are held in low esteem by ecologists because they usurp habitats that normally would be occupied by less aggressive native species, and some, although edible and maybe delicious, are too endangered — or too pretty — to consider picking. Some plants, such as daylilies and Jerusalem artichokes, actually benefit by a little thinning. So pick away, but leave enough for animals — or other humans if you are not on your own land.

Each plant is ranked: The higher the grade, the less one need worry about any adverse ecological impact from harvesting it.

A+ *Exceedingly common, mostly alien, and often invasive species generally held in low regard by ecologists. Picking these plants is unlikely to make a dent in their ability to perpetuate themselves. Pick as many as you can.*

A *Common introduced and native species that are plentiful enough to harvest without impact on their availability for future harvests.*

A- *Common, mostly introduced species, usually found in small patches. Care should be taken to ensure that enough plants are left after harvesting so the plant may continue to exist in that location.*

B+ *Very common, mostly native species found in good-sized patches where they are often relied upon by native fauna for food. These plants are usually numerous enough to be harvested for as much as one needs.*

B *Locally abundant native species plus a few aliens that tend to be particular about the type of habitat in which they will grow. Take care to leave plenty so they will continue to thrive.*

B- *Elusive plants appearing only in a small portion of the habitat that is suitable for them. Occasionally they can be found in large patches, but even then care must be taken to harvest lightly and not endanger their ability to thrive in that location.*

C+ *Rare enough that careless harvesting could harm them. Only one of every dozen plants should be taken.*

C *Rare and confined to very specialized habitats, or more common but considered too pretty to pick.*

C- *Rare native wildflowers or species that should not be picked.*

B- Arrowhead
A- Barberry
B Bayberry
B Beach Pea
C+ Beach Plum
B+ Beech
B+ Blackberry
B Black Walnut
B+ Blueberry
A+ Bracken Fern
A+ Burdock
B Butternut
A Cattail
C Chestnut
A+ Chicory
B+ Carragheen/Irish Moss
B+ Clintonia
A Clover
A Coltsfoot
B Cranberry
B Ground Cherry
A+ Oxeye Daisy
A+ Dandelion
A Daylily
B+ Elderberry
B- Ostrich Fern
B Fireweed
A Foxtail Grass
B+ Glasswort
B+ Sweet Goldenrod
B+ Hawthorn
B Hazelnut
B+ Jerusalem Artichoke
B+ Jewelweed
B+ Kelp
A+ Lamb's-quarters
A- Linden Tree
A Mallow
B+ Maple
C Marsh Marigold
A+ Milkweed
A+ Mulberry
A Nettle
A+ Plantain
B+ Pokeweed
B+ Raspberry
B+ Sassafras
B+ Sea Rocket
B+ Shagbark Hickory
A+ Sheep Sorrel
A+ Sumac
C- Trillium
C- Trout Lily
A Watercress
B+ White Oak
B- Wild Asparagus
A+ Wild Carrot
C+ Wild Ginger
C+ Wild Leek
B+ Wild Mint
B- Wild Rice
A Wild Rose
B+ Wild Strawberry
B+ Wintergreen
A+ Wood Sorrel

Right: a display of drying herbs, seaweeds, and fungi

Enjoy your Weeds

A wise old countryman said, "All plants, when they take their food from the soil, are bound to take the minerals in the soil, and that mineral varies with different plants. Watercress, now, took up a lot of iron, and broom and gorse took up sulphur, so you used the plant itself. Chemists are so clever they get the minerals out of the soil direct, but as we are animals, and plants come between us and the minerals, it does make sense to let the vegetables digest the minerals before we use them."

Feverfew
Tea from this plant, a perennial with small, daisylike flowers, has long been given for colds, fevers, arthritis, and other ailments.

Ramp *or* Wild Leek
A choice wild food found in moist, rich woods. It has a white bulb that looks and tastes much like a small leek. It is wonderful either cooked or pickled, and has the same healing and health properties ascribed to onions and garlic.

Pokeweed
Only the young spring shoots (under six inches) are safe to eat; all other parts are poisonous. However, berry teas and root poultices have been used by skilled practitioners in Native American and folk medicine.

Common Plantain
Introduced from Europe, this lawn weed is edible as a salad green or vegetable when the leaves are very young. In folk medicine it is believed to stimulate internal and external healing.

Jewelweed

Both the orange and yellow-flowered jewelweed are annuals whose tender shoots can be eaten before they exceed five inches. The crushed leaves are used for poison ivy rash and other skin problems

Common Cattail

Early young shoots, peeled of their coarse outer rind, cooked and served with butter, are a delicacy often called "Cossack asparagus."

Yarrow

Herbal tea made from the dried leaves is said to be a tonic and a remedy for colds, fevers, and internal disorders.

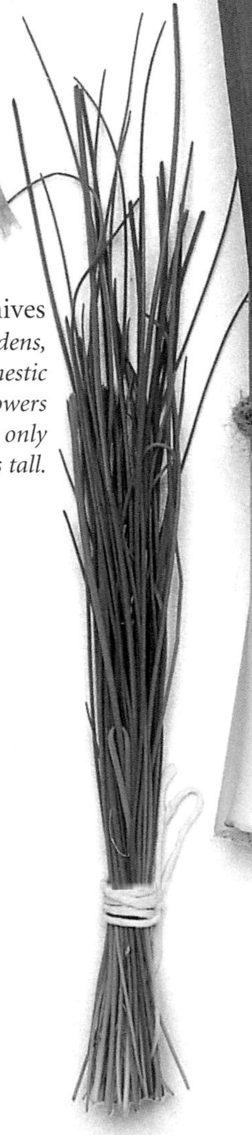

Wild Chives

Escapees from gardens, wild chives, like their domestic cousins, have lavender flowers and hollow leaves, but are only about six inches tall.

Winter cress

Introduced from Europe, this member of the mustard family is found in wet fields. The young leaves are good in salads or cooked like spinach, and were once used as a poultice on wounds.

Spring-Beauty *or* Fairy Spuds

After the small (one inch) tubers are boiled and the tough jackets peeled, they can be served like potatoes.

I was staying with some French friends who lived in the hills above Lyons, when early one morning my host handed me a small kitchen knife "with all the aplomb," as Calvin Trillin once said, "of an English squire loaning a guest his favorite walking stick." He told me we were going to get breakfast. Off we went in the car up into a valley where, in a large meadow, there were already small groups of people on their dew-covered knees.

Our task was to find baby dandelion leaves and remove them as close to the ground as possible. The fine, white leaf stalks, I was told, had the most delicate flavor. Also, as the plant grew, the shaded leaves were less bitter. When we returned, my friend made a wonderful salad from the dandelion leaves, and topped it with croutons and chopped ham. Cheese omelets and fresh bread completed our morning meal.

Common dandelion

(Taraxacum officinale)

The dandelion, a perennial, is so admired that entire books have been written celebrating its use in everything from soups and salads to "coffee" and desserts to herbal medicines. This beautiful weed, with its bright yellow flowers, was introduced to North America by European settlers. It is generally believed that its name was derived from the French *dent de lion* (lion's tooth) referring to the toothed edges of the leaves. It is remarkable because every part except the stem can be used as a food or medicine: the young leaves are eaten raw in salads or cooked as a vegetable; the roots can be prepared as any root vegetable or roasted and used as a coffee substitute; the flowers are used to make beer or wine or dipped in batter and fried. In the early days of medicine, even before much was known about vitamins, the leaves (high in vitamins A and C) were eaten as a spring tonic; teas from the roots and leaves were prescribed for all manner of internal problems.

Dandelion wine has a fine, sharp flavor with just a hint of resin, like a mild Retsina.

Dandelion Wine

16 cups dandelion flowers (all green parts removed)
3 pounds granulated sugar
2 oranges
1 lemon
1 tablespoon active dry yeast
4 quarts boiling water

1. Put the flowers in a large, nonreactive pot and add boiling water. Let sit for three days, then strain through cheesecloth.
2. Add sugar, grated orange and lemon rind, and juices to the strained liquid and boil to make a syrup. Cool to lukewarm and add yeast.
4. Let mixture stand for four days in a warm room, covered lightly with plastic wrap.
5. Filter the liquid into a nonreactive container. Cover loosely and let sit until fermentation stops, about three weeks. Funnel into sterilized wine bottles, cork tightly, and store in a cool, dark place for about six months before serving.

Yield: 4 quarts

Ostrich Fern (*Matteuccia Struthiopteris*)
Fiddlehead Fern

Fiddleheads are not a species but an early stage of spring growth when the fronds are young and curled. Several species are edible, but the ostrich fern is considered choice. It is the one you are most likely to see in greenmarkets and specialty stores. Ferns thrive in rich, wet soil, growing in clumps from rhizomes. Once you have marked their location, be very attentive to their growth, because the emerald-green fiddleheads, covered with dry, brown scales, must be picked when they are no more than six inches high and still tightly coiled. If you miss the moment, they grow increasingly tough and bitter, soon becoming unfit for human consumption, i.e., poisonous. Also, protect your source by picking only half of any clump. Leave the other half to supply energy to the rhizomes for next year's crop.

Other edibles are the cinnamon fern (*Osmunda cinnamomea)*, shaped like the ostrich fern, and bracken (*Pteridium aquilinum)*, which has a fiddlehead shaped like an eagle's claw and is covered with silver-gray fuzz that can be rubbed off. Bracken grows in sunny, open places. There have been studies exploring possible cancer-causing substances in bracken, but it is generally believed that bracken fiddleheads eaten in small quantities in spring are not harmful. As with other fiddleheads, they should be picked and eaten only when the fronds are tightly curled.

If you've never eaten fiddleheads, you might wonder why they are so special. I suppose it has a lot to do with the excitement of smelling the earth and picking fresh greens with the grassy taste of spring; they remind me of asparagus and need to be cooked just as carefully. First gently rub off the protective scales with your fingers, or soak the fiddleheads in water until most of the scales float off. Then trim the stems and blanch the ferns in salted, boiling water until tender yet crunchy. They can be tossed with butter and salt or a vinaigrette made with mild vinegar. They can be used as well in numerous recipes of your choice.

Ferns have other uses, too. When I went camping as a kid in the cold English autumn, we stacked bracken around the outside of our tent and stuffed it under our bedding for insulation. Thomas Jefferson, after strolling in the forest of Fontainebleau, wrote, ". . . [I] saw a man cutting fern. I went to him under the pretense of asking the shortest road to the town, and afterwards asked for what use he was cutting fern. He told me that this part of the country furnished a great deal of fruit to Paris. That when packed in straw it acquired an ill taste, but that dry fern preserved it perfectly without communicating any taste at all. I treasured this observation for the preservation of my apples on my return to my own country."

The young bud photographed in early April

Gently does it. The lower part of the stalk can come away if jerked.

The flower in early summer

Ramp or Wild Leek (*Allium tricoccum*)

Guidebooks always say wild leeks grow in rich, moist soil in the woods. This is true, but be warned that in a wet spring, or downhill from snowmelt, you will need to wear rubber boots when you harvest them. It also will help to have a garden trowel along to remove the ramps neatly. If you simply pull the plant, the little white bulbs are likely to remain in the ground and you will be left holding a handful of leaves. Wild leeks send up green leaves in the spring that, as they unroll, are flat and lance-shaped, from one to three inches wide and five to nine inches long. Ramps grow in patches, and you probably will smell them before you actually spot the leaves. Later, in June or July, the leaves wither, and a stalk bearing whitish flowers will mark their place.

Ramps are mild tasting, a bit like the garden leek although strong smelling, and are generally considered to be the best wild onion. In fact, they are so highly regarded that spring "ramp festivals," where they are cooked in many ways, are held in West Virginia. Last spring, we tried pickling them in the style of British pub onions and were very pleased with the results. We substituted a milder vinegar for traditional malt vinegar so that the delicately flavored ramps would not be overwhelmed.

Pickled Ramps

4 pounds ramp bulbs
3 tablespoons pickling salt, or other salt without iodine
4 bay leaves
2 teaspoons black peppercorns
2 teaspoons whole allspice
1 teaspoon hot red pepper flakes
2 teaspoons pickling salt
4 cups cider vinegar
2 cups rice-wine vinegar
4-6 pint canning jars and lids, sterilized

1. Wash the ramps thoroughly, remove the green tops and roots, and rinse in clean water. Place in a nonreactive ceramic or stainless-steel bowl, stir in three tablespoons of pickling salt and cover. Let stand overnight.
2. Combine the two teaspoons salt, spices, and vinegars in a nonreactive saucepan. Bring to a boil and simmer for five minutes. Remove from heat, cool and let rest until you are ready to put the ramps into canning jars.
3. Rinse salt from ramps in large bowl of cold water. Drain and repeat three times.
4. Place ramps in a colander and drain. Roll them in paper towels until most of the water has been absorbed.
5. Strain the pickling solution into a large, nonreactive pot and bring to a boil. Add the ramp bulbs, lower to a simmer, and cook for three minutes. Remove from heat.
6. Immediately ladle ramps and liquid into hot, sterilized canning jars. Make sure bulbs are covered by one-half inch of pickling solution. Seal with sterilized lids. Store in a cool place and let them mellow for at least a month before using.

Yield: 4-6 pints

Common Cattail (*Typha latifolia*)

These tall, spiked perennials grow in swampy or marshy land throughout North America. They spread rapidly. After the plants emerge from the water, they may grow as much as three inches a day, reaching a height ranging from eight to fifteen feet. Once fertilized, the female flower turns into the brown "hot dog," a shape familiar in the country landscape. Cattails are special in that the entire plant is either edible or usable in some way.

In spring, the swollen sprouts can be dug from the mud and eaten raw or cooked. A few weeks later, tender shoots, often called "Cossack asparagus," begin to appear. After the tough outer leaves are removed, the greenish core can be cooked or eaten raw in salads. Soon golden pollen from the flower heads can be shaken into a paper bag and used like flour for pancakes and muffins. Later the roots can be cooked and eaten like potatoes, or dried and made into a high-starch flour.

Cossack Asparagus

24 twelve-inch cattail shoots
2-4 tablespoons butter
Salt and pepper

1. Trim the bottoms and tops of shoots and peel off the coarse outer leaves. A pale green-white core about ten inches long will remain. (It will look a bit like a thin leek.)
2. Place in a large, nonreactive frying pan and cover with water. Bring to a boil, reduce heat to medium, and cook until tender but firm. Do not overcook or the shoots will become mushy.
3. Drain and dress with butter, salt, and pepper to taste.

The leaves of the cattail can be used for chair seats, the rushes for weaving mats and roofs, and the fluff inside the flower heads to stuff pillows. Native Americans poulticed the pounded root on wounds, sores, and burns; and the root infused in milk has been used to relieve dysentery and diarrhea.

Oxeye Daisy (*Chrysanthemum Leucanthemum*)

This daisy, seen everywhere in summer, has small flowers (about two inches across) featuring a yellow center and white petals. Its leaves, when young and light green, can be added to salads.

Wild Chamomile (*Matricaria Chamomilla*)

Brought to North America by Europeans for their gardens, this annual escaped and is now widely seen in fields and along roadsides. It is apple scented with small, daisylike flowers. The stems grow from six to twenty-four inches tall. The dried flowers are steeped to make a fragrant, pale gold tea traditionally used to relieve insomnia, indigestion, headaches, colds, fever, colic, and arthritis.

Wild Ginger *(Asarum canadense)*

A beautiful plant with twin heart-shaped leaves, wild ginger puts up a small, dark red flower just between its leaves in spring. This is the time to mark the spot in the woods, where it usually grows, so you can come back in the fall to collect the roots when they are at their best. The thin roots grow horizontally just under the surface, thus giving rise to its common name, "snakeroot."

Although not related to tropical ginger, wild ginger has a similar taste and smell, and early settlers dried its root to use as a substitute. You can do the same by washing and slicing the roots and drying them in a dehydrator until crisp. Or, alternately, place them in a 200°F oven for two to three hours. Fresh ginger root is excellent for use in candy, syrups, and drinks.

Wintergreen (*Gaultheria procumbens*)

This low-growing evergreen creeps along the ground in poor or acidic soil, often under conifers in the Northeast. It has the familiar wintergreen fragrance, and its shiny, dark green leaves are attached to the tops of short stems, where white, bell-shaped flowers appear in summer followed by bright red edible berries. Fresh, chopped leaves steeped in boiling water make a refreshing tea that can later be used as a mouthwash. One also can refresh the mouth and soothe irritated gums by chewing the leaves or eating the berries.

Fireweed (*Epilobium angustifolium*)

As you might guess, fireweed grows very well and spreads rapidly on burned lands. It is a tall perennial with showy, rose-to-purple flowers valuable for honey, and lance-shaped leaves. In some areas it is referred to as "wild asparagus" because the young spring shoots can be prepared like asparagus. The young leaves, like spinach, can be eaten as a salad or a cooked vegetable. As with many other plants, the taste grows bitter as the plant matures. The mature leaves can be dried and used to make tea, a folk remedy for dysentery and abdominal cramps. The Native Americans reportedly poulticed the peeled root on burns.

Chicory (*Cichorium intybus*)

During the Civil War when blockades kept many goods from entering Southern ports, chicory root served as a substitute for coffee beans. The fleshy white taproots of the chicory plants are dug up in late summer and roasted slowly until crisp. They are then cut into pieces and ground in a coffee grinder. Many people like chicory's strong taste, and it is an important ingredient today in New Orleans Creole coffee.

Growing from the root is a one-to four-foot stem with small, intense blue flowers. The flowers on individual plants bloom sequentially, but each one lasts only a day. This import from Europe and Asia escaped from gardens and now grows throughout the country in fields and on roadsides. Its young leaves can be used in salads or as a vegetable, but older leaves are bitter.

Chicory flowers are a rough guide to telling the time of day. During its day-long life, each flower closes up at noon for a short period.

Coltsfoot (*Tussilago farfara*)

Coltsfoot is the first wildflower to appear along our dirt road in spring after the ground has thawed. It usually grows on the sides of the drainage ditches closest to the road, where it gets the most light. On a sunny day, the yellow, dandelion-like flowers open and coltsfoot seems to be everywhere, but on a cloudy, rainy day, they close so tightly they are almost invisible. A single flower tops the scaly, reddish stem, which usually has withered by the time the leaves appear. The heart-shaped, jagged leaves were thought to resemble a colt's hoofprint, giving this perennial its common name.

Coltsfoot's generic name comes from the Latin words *tussis ago*, "I drive (out) a cough," relating to the fact that this European import has been used by healers since the earliest times as a remedy for coughs, colds, asthma, bronchitis, and sore throats. The common methods of using coltsfoot include drinking tea from the leaves, smoking the crushed, dried leaves in a pipe, and making the rootstock into candied cough drops. All are believed to be effective in loosening phlegm and relieving a persistent cough. Considered a medicinal herb, coltsfoot has culinary uses as well. Wine or beer can be made from its flowers, and the young leaves can be sauteed or steamed as a vegetable.

In the summer you will see patches of wild day lilies, usually orange or yellow, growing along roadsides all over the country.

Daylily (*Hemerocallis fulva*)

Daylilies escaped from cultivation, but flourished because they were able to adapt easily to a wide variety of soil and climatic conditions. Each flower remains open only for a day, hence the Greek name, *hemerocallis,* meaning "beautiful for a day." The plants keep blooming for weeks in the summer, however, providing an almost constant supply of buds and flowers.

Many foragers consider the buds the most delicious edible part of the plant. Buds should be gathered while small and green and simmered for about ten minutes in salted water. They are then ready to be tossed in butter or a vinaigrette, or sauteed with garlic and summer herbs. The fresh flowers are a delight when dipped in a batter — like zucchini flowers — and fried; and the dried flowers have long been a part of Chinese cuisine. The late fall is a good time to dig up some of your daylily tubers to be replanted elsewhere, or simply to thin out existing plants for better growth the following summer. The small tubers also can be eaten raw or cooked.

Watercress *(Nasturtium officinale)*

You will recognize watercress easily in the wild: the dark green leaves look much like the domestic variety sold in the supermarket. A member of the mustard family, it is a hardy perennial with a peppery bite that does best in gently flowing water. It grows almost everywhere in the United States but likes cool water better than warm, so winter is its best season in the South. After you locate a nearby clump of watercress, investigate your water — even have it tested — to check for pollution and use by cows and other animals. Once you have determined that the water is safe, you can harvest either before the white flowers appear or in the fall, by cutting just under the waterline. Thoroughly wash the watercress and, if you have concerns, eat it cooked instead of raw.

The fresh leaves are high in vitamins A and C and iodine, and traditionally have been used as a tonic and for rheumatism, heart trouble, goiter, and scurvy (one of its common names is scurvy grass).

Watercress Soup

2 tablespoons butter
1 small onion, finely chopped
4 medium potatoes
6 cups chicken stock
Salt and pepper
1/8 teaspoon fresh grated nutmeg
2 bunches of watercress
1/2 cup heavy cream

1. *Melt butter in large pot and cook onion until translucent. Add potatoes, stock, and seasonings. Simmer until the potatoes are cooked.*
2. *Cut watercress leaves from the thick bottom stems. Wash thoroughly.*
3. *In batches, puree the potatoes, onions and liquid with the watercress in a food processor.*
4. *Return soup to the pot, adding more stock if too thick, and reheat without boiling. Check seasonings, add cream, and serve.*

Serves 4-6, or 10 cups

Ground Cherry *(Physalis species)*

There are many species of the ground cherry, commonly called Japanese or Chinese lantern, husk tomato, or clammy or Virginia ground cherry, that have an edible fruit enclosed in a lanternlike husk. The generic name is derived from the Greek *phusa*, "a bladder," referring to the way the calyx inflates and encloses the fruit after the petals have fallen off. The small berry is ready in late summer or early fall when the husk becomes brown and papery. It can be eaten in jams and pies, or relishes and salsas. Be sure of your identification, since it belongs to the nightshade family and has unpleasant relatives.

All wild rose hips have twenty times more vitamin C than oranges. These are Rosa Eglantaria *hips, the Sweetbrier.*

Wrinkled Rose (*Rosa rugosa*)

You are probably familiar with the beauty and scent of wild roses, and you know they grow on thorny shrubs. But you may not have given much thought to their food and medicinal value. This comes from the fruits known as rose hips, or haws, which are very high in vitamin C and have been used for centuries in herbal medicines to reduce infection. Rose hips ripen in the fall and vary in size. They are best picked after the first frost, which softens the texture and sweetens the taste of the fruit. One of the best wild roses for harvesting is the wrinkled, or rugosa, rose, which has an especially large hip. This rose, found along the seashore dunes or roadsides, has five-petaled flowers and dark-green, wrinkled leaves. Sometimes it is actually planted to help hold back dunes or dirt banks. Before cooking, the hips should be cut in half and the seeds in the center scooped out. Since they are high in pectin, rose hips make good jams and jellies.

The oil from rose petals has traditionally been infused into water and applied as a perfume or an astringent. Rose water was also a very popular ingredient in various natural cosmetics when ladies made their own. My wife even remembers her grandmother mixing rose water and glycerin and putting it on her skin to keep it soft.

Edible seaweeds are full of gelatin, which is the perfect diet food. It has bulk, nutrients, few calories, and is easily digestible. Gelatins from animals have eighty times the calories of those from seaweed.

Slender Glasswort or Samphire

(*Salicornia europaea*)

It is interesting to note that this plant is high in soda; in times past it was collected from coastal marshes or wet alkaline inland spots for use in making soap and glass. Now we search it out as a treat for its delicate, salty flavor. In spring and early summer you will see a bed of emerald green or pink spikes poking up, followed by succulent jointed stems branching from near the base. At this point it looks like "chicken claws," one of its popular common names. Glasswort is usually picked at low tide and is best eaten soon thereafter, although it will keep in the refrigerator for a couple of days. The early spring shoots can be eaten raw in salads, and the larger ones are delicious either cooked or pickled in a mild vinegar.
I can remember years ago when samphire was sold in pickle jars or served steamed with crabs. Then fashions changed, and it was forgotten. But now, in more health-conscious times, it has made a comeback and is considered a luxury. One recent summer in East Anglia, a very good village seafood store had a sign in the window saying, "Sorry, Samphire Sold Out."

Cooked Glasswort

1. *Wash the glasswort, leaving the roots intact, and tie in bunches.*
2. *Boil in unsalted water for eight to ten minutes. Remove from the pot, drain, and cut the string.*
3. *Place in a serving dish and dress with melted butter and pepper.*
4. *Each stem contains a woody stalk. Pick the glasswort up by the root and bite the stem, gently pulling the fleshy part from the woody center.*

Mesquite *(Prosopis glandulosa)*

The Native Americans of the Southwest, where the mesquite thrives because of its massive root system, have made good use of this small tree over the centuries. On its spreading branches, appearing on rounded spikes, are small, green flowers, delightfully sugary to suck, followed by tender pods that can be cooked and served as a vegetable. Dried and ground, the seeds make meal that can be used in breads and puddings or stored for winter use. Mesquite seeds also have served as animal feed; the bark has been turned into skirts, twine, and baskets.

Pinyon Pine (*Pinus edulis*)

The soft, small nuts of all the Pinus species growing in the western United States and Mexico are edible but vary in quality. Pine nuts are high in protein and fatty oil (3202 calories to the pound!). The seeds were removed from the cones in quantities by Native Americans, who stored them for the winter. They also raided the nests of pack rats to get at their stashes. Nuts from *Pinus edulis* are generally considered to be the tastiest, especially when roasted. Ground into flour, pine nuts can be added for body and flavor to everything from pancakes and cakes to soups and stews.

Edward Abbey said in *Desert Solitaire,* "... Pine nuts are delicious, sweeter than hazelnuts but difficult to eat; you have to crack the shells in your teeth and then, because they are smaller than peanut kernels, you have to separate the meat from the shell with your tongue. If one had to spend a winter ... with nothing to eat but pinyon nuts, it is an interesting question whether or not you could eat them fast enough to keep from starving to death."

There have been stories of "foodies" in Europe falling out of trees similar to pinyon pine during desperate attempts to get at *pignolis* for their fresh pesto.

The remarkable pinyon was used in many ways by the Native Americans — for its resin to waterproof baskets and relieve rheumatism, sore throats, and boils; for its needles to make tea; and for its inner bark and young wood eaten as trail food.

Mushrooms

In the summer, I can rarely go for a walk without turning it into a foray, and from the first week of July onward I'm after mushrooms. After ten years I know where the spots are, so all I wish for is at least one day a week with a good rainfall. We are lucky to have a field bordered on its north side with mature oak trees stretching for about a quarter of a mile. Under the circle of their branches, on mossy, grassy ground, yellow chanterelles grow, smelling like apricots. They obviously like the diffused shade. They do not pop up like the bigger-capped mushrooms but are closer to the ground, sometimes hiding under thick grass and leaves. When you find one, you will spot others nearby, and when you get down nearer to their level, your eye begins to sharpen and you'll find more and more. Chanterelles, like most other ground fungi, grow in a ring, and you'll soon recognize which way the ring is curving.

Sometimes I find large clumps of black chanterelles, which prefer a little more gloom and a layer of dead leaves to push through. They never, in my experience, reappear in the same place, and they are hard to see, but finding one means finding them all. They seem to escape the attention of slugs, too. At the same time, among the less-edible boletes, I have found choice ceps. Getting them before the slugs do means an early start.

I'm unsure of the mushroom cycle, so I always leave some unpicked. When I remember them, I spread dry cow manure in places that have been good to me.

Before we get to particular species and ways to serve them, here are some words of caution. Most mushrooms are not dangerous, even if not worth tasting, but some are *extremely dangerous* to eat. I have been over-cautious, and although often proved wrong, I'll probably remain that way. To avoid ever getting mixed up with the pure-looking, white and deadly *Amanita* family — including the Death Cap — I avoid all mushrooms that are white with white gills underneath.

Years ago, I found an enormous ring of very large brown-capped mushrooms that ranged in size from that of buns to small loaves. They smelled and looked good, so I sliced through one. Its stalk and gills began to turn green, then azure. I checked through my guides, made a spore print, and was convinced that it was not poisonous. But that color change did me in — it just didn't seem right, so I threw the mushrooms away. After checking the deposit from the spores the following season, I found out that what I did not have the nerve for turned out to be delicious yellow-cracked boletes.

Last year in early fall, I went on a fungi walk conducted at a nearby environmental preserve. It was to be led by a mycologist who was, I found, replaced by an amateur. The morning did little to add to my knowledge of fungi. Before embarking on the stroll, our leader gathered us around his well-thumbed guidebook and told us never to look at mushrooms printed in color because the printing is never accurate. One sensible thing he did say was that making a spore print was the safest way to understand a mushroom. During the walk he admitted that a mushroom's color meant little to him because he was colorblind. I left about then, certain that the colors of a spore print would confuse him further. Here is what sensible gatherers and mycologists say:

Never eat any mushroom unless you can absolutely identify it as edible.

Buy several good reference guides such as *The Audubon Society Field Guide to North American Mushrooms* or Roger Phillips' *Mushrooms of North America* (which is well-printed in color with accurate scale markings) and use at least two for positive identification. If you have any doubts, take sample mushrooms to an expert in your area.

Be warned. Looking like a pile of freshly baked brioches, this tasty-looking clump is made up of poisonous Jack O'Lanterns. They were growing out of the base of a dead tree on a bank of our pond. When I went back to the spot at night, they were glowing a pale green. Imagine these in your stomach!

Yellow Chanterelle *(Cantharellus cibarius)*

The summer we moved to the country, I immediately began walking about our fields and woods searching for mushrooms. At first I found none, but within a few days there was a heavy downpour that I hoped would cause some to appear. So I put on my boots and, with high expectations, went out to our long, mown field bordered with oaks and conifers. And there they were under the oaks — bright yellow chanterelles, smelling slightly of apricots, looking like spilled egg yolks. I picked one or two and ran back to the house to show them to my wife. She insisted that I prove they were not the poisonous Jack O'Lanterns, which I did with the help of my best field guides. Chanterelles are found in July and August in the Northeast, from September to November and later in the Northwest. If you have located a spot where some might grow, go out early in the morning after a rain and pick them before the slugs get busy. Since these mushrooms push up through the ground, they usually need to be rinsed under cold running water to remove dirt. Large, older ones should be sliced down the middle to remove any little invaders.

Our yellow chanterelles keep appearing every year in the same places. One very rainy summer we had such an enormous quantity that even after giving them to our friends and preparing all sorts of recipes, we had enough left to dry and freeze. We found that complicated recipes tend to obscure the delicate taste of chanterelles, so we stick with the following simple one. We serve it, with a dry white wine, for lunch accompanied by a green salad or as a first course at dinner. My favorite moment in the enjoyment of this recipe is when the flavor of the chanterelles and herbs combine in the juices soaked into the toasted French bread.

Chanterelles with Herbs

8 1/4 inch slices French bread
2 tablespoons olive oil
2 tablespoons unsalted butter
6 cups fresh chanterelles, cleaned, pulled apart lengthwise in 2-4 pieces, depending on size
1/4 cup chives, chopped
1/2 cup mixed fresh herbs, chopped (summer savory, tarragon, thyme, oregano)
1/2 cup fresh parsley, chopped
1 teaspoon salt, or to taste
Freshly ground black pepper

1. *Toast bread and place two slices on each of four warmed plates.*
2. *In a twelve-inch skillet, heat butter and oil until bubbling. Add mushrooms and cook over medium-high heat, tossing frequently for about four minutes, or until soft. The mushrooms will release a good amount of juice.*
3. *Add the chives, herbs, parsley, and salt and toss to blend for about one minute.*
4. *Spoon the mushroom mixture with its juices over the toast. Top with freshly ground pepper and serve immediately.*

Yield: 4 servings

My best spots for finding chanterelles and ceps are under the low branches on the north side of mature oak trees. I go over the area lightly with a scythe — just enough to keep down the brush.

You have to get down low when there is thick grass. The chanterelles are hard to see at first, but you'll soon develop a sense of where they are likely to be, and you can also pick up their scent — it's just like apricots.

A camper's feast. Here the chanterelles are sauteed with cured ham, a precooked potato, and a handful of parsley.

Giant Puffball

(*Calvatia gigantea*)

It is absolutely amazing to happen upon a puffball — especially a large one. They seem so perfect and white sitting there on a lawn, or in a meadow or old pasture. Common from summer to late fall, they are usually between eight and fifteen inches across, though there have been reports of huge puffballs weighing many pounds. Puffballs are choice edibles only while the flesh is snow white and firm; they become bitter as they age and a tinge of yellow appears. Slice small puffballs from top to bottom to make sure there is no outline of a stem or gills, which would mean you accidentally picked up a poisonous *Amanita*. There are many ways to cook puffballs: for a low-fat version, try slices brushed lightly with olive oil and baked; or for an Oriental style, dip slices in tempura batter, deep fry, and serve with sauce.

Sauteed Puffballs

2 tablespoons canola oil
2 tablespoons butter
1 small puffball, sliced
1/2 cup flour
1 egg, beaten
1/2 teaspoon salt
1 cup fresh bread crumbs
1/4 cup grated parmesan cheese

1. *Heat oil and butter in skillet until bubbling.*
2. *Dust mushroom slices with flour and shake off excess.*
3. *Dip into beaten egg and salt, then press both sides gently into mixture of bread crumbs and parmesan.*
4. *Add enough slices to cover bottom of skillet without crowding, cook quickly until golden brown, and drain on paper towels. Repeat until all slices are cooked. Serve hot.*

Serves 2

Yellow Morel (*Morchella esculenta*)

Mushroom foragers are almost always secretive about places where they find their prizes — especially about where they find morels, which have a very short season, seldom more than a month. Morels require a near-perfect combination of temperature and moisture to produce abundantly. They occur from March to June, growing either singly or in groups in burned-over spots, old apple orchards, and under ashes, oaks, beeches, and maples. I have the best luck when the apple trees are just losing their blossoms. Morels are distinguished by their cream to brownish yellow, conical and honeycombed cap, and by the fact that both the cap and stalk are hollow. There is also an edible black morel (*Morchella elata*). You must carefully check the morels you find to be certain they are true morels: "false" morels are similar in appearance to the edible but contain toxins that render them dangerous.

If you find a quantity of morels, refrigerate them or start drying them immediately. Otherwise, rot will set in quickly. Morels need to be prepared before cooking to make sure no little creatures are in the cavities. Slice them in half from top to bottom, trim the stems, and rinse under cold running water. Drop them into boiling water for two minutes to blanch, then dry them on paper towels.

Dry morels by cutting them in half, trimming the base of the stem, and rinsing under cold running water. Afterwards, dry on paper towels, thread on strings, and hang them up to dry in a warm spot. Store in sterilized canning jars with clean tops. When ready to use, blanch for two minutes in boiling, salted water.

Morels in Cream

6-8 large, fresh morels
1 tablespoon unsalted butter
1/2 teaspoon chopped garlic
1/2 cup heavy cream
1 tablespoon chopped parsley
1/2 teaspoon salt and pepper, or to taste

1. Prepare fresh morels as directed above. Cut into large pieces, saute in butter for three to four minutes.
2. Add garlic and cook for two minutes.
3. Add cream, parsley, salt, and pepper and simmer for five to ten minutes.

Good with grilled polenta or pasta.

Serves 2-4

Cep or King Bolete

(*Boletus edulis*)

This mushroom, prized for its flavor and texture, is large with a reddish-brown cap that sometimes grows up to ten inches around and a stem that thickens toward the base. The generic name, *Boletus*, comes from the Greek word *bolus*, meaning lump. You can look for ceps on the ground under conifers and deciduous trees from June to October. Edible young ceps have white pores under the cap; as they age, the pores turn yellow and must be peeled away from the cap and discarded. Although excellent fresh, boletes may be preserved for the winter by washing them carefully, slicing, and placing them in the sun or in a food dryer. When reconstituting dried mushrooms, carefully remove the mushroom pieces, then strain the liquid to remove any sediment or grit. You will be able to find many recipes using both fresh and dried ceps, but the following is excellent for revealing the taste without a lot of fuss. You also can create a marinade using different herbs, soy sauce, etc., to suit the character of your meal.

Grilled Ceps

Oil for grill
2 large ceps
4 tablespoons olive oil
2 tablespoons balsamic vinegar
1/2 teaspoon salt

1. Prepare a gas or charcoal grill. When ready to cook, oil the grill.
2. Clean mushrooms and remove stems.
Leave the caps whole and slice the stems in half lengthwise. Place in a shallow dish.
3. Whisk together oil, vinegar, and salt and pour over caps and stems. Marinate for twenty minutes, turning several times.
4. Remove from marinade and grill for approximately four minutes on each side.

Serves 4

Black Trumpet (*Craterellus fallax*)

We rarely find black chanterelles in our area because of the temperature and rainfall. However, every year we patrol our property, searching under beeches, oaks, and other deciduous trees. When we find them, they are in a big clump several square yards across. Dark gray to black, and small — 3/8 to 3 1/4 inches wide — these trumpet-shaped mushrooms are well camouflaged by the color of the earth and by fallen leaves so that one must look quite carefully. Found throughout North America from June to November, black trumpets have a delightfully woodsy taste and smell, both fresh and dried. The first time I reconstituted these dried mushrooms,I was delighted to find they still had a strong odor and flavor.

Gnocchi with Black Trumpets

1 1/2 pounds mixed fresh mushrooms: black trumpets, meadow mushrooms, and ceps
1 tablespoon unsalted butter
2 cloves garlic, peeled and minced
1 cup unsalted chicken stock
1/2 cup cream
2 tablespoons chopped chives
Salt and freshly ground pepper
1 pound gnocchi

1. Clean black trumpets and trim ends; remove stems from meadow mushrooms or ceps and reserve for another use. Cut caps into 1/4-inch slices.
2. Melt butter in large skillet. Add garlic and saute four minutes over low heat. Add mushrooms and cook until they release their liquid. Add chicken stock and simmer for five minutes. Stir in cream and simmer for another five minutes. Add salt and pepper to taste.
3. Boil the gnocchi until tender but firm, and drain. Toss with the mushrooms and garnish with chives.

Serves 4 as a first course.

Meadow or Common Field Mushroom

(*Agaricus campestris*)

These mushrooms start popping up on lawns and mown meadows in our part of the country in late August and sometimes last as late as October. In warmer parts of the country they can continue on into winter. When out driving, we keep a bag in the car just in case we spot some along our route. (Visiting friends often think we have gone crazy when we stop suddenly for no apparent reason and dash out of the car.) The cap of this mushroom is smooth and whitish and the gills begin as pink, later turning chocolate to blackish brown. Another similar-looking choice edible is the horse mushroom (*Agaricus arvensis*), which is larger, bruises yellow, and smells of anise when young.

Note: Because the deadly white *Amanitas* grow in similar habitats, you must be positive about your identification. The photograph above is particularly useful. Although we picked these at the same time, you can see the difference in gill color between the smaller, younger ones and the larger, mature ones. The *Amanita phalloides*, or Death Cap, looks just like these from above, but its gills are white.

The field mushroom is a relative of the cultivated white button mushroom but with a stronger, nuttier taste, so that you can substitute it in your favorite recipes. In a good wet year, there may be so many mushrooms that you will want to save some for the winter. From our experience, we feel freezing is better than drying. Frozen mushrooms can be used in many ways. Following is our method:

Mushroom Preparation for Freezing

3 to 4 pounds field mushrooms

1. *Cut off the soil-covered ends of stems. Clean mushrooms as thoroughly as possible, but do not soak in water.*
2. *Chop mushroom caps and stems very coarsely, and place in a metal colander.*
3. *Pour about an inch of water in the bottom of a large pot. In the center of the pot place a stainless-steel bowl wide enough to catch drippings from the bottom of the colander.*
4. *Rest the colander on top of the pot and cover with aluminum foil.*
5. *Bring the water to a boil and steam for ten minutes, stirring after five minutes.*
6. *Remove colander with mushrooms from pot and set aside. Strain juices from the bowl to get rid of any grit.*
7. *Add mushrooms to strained juices, place in containers, and freeze.*

Yield: 4-6 cups

Maple syrup can be extracted from several species of maple tree. In the North and East and as far west as the prairies it's the sugar, black, or rock maple; silver, or white, maple; and the box elder. Farther on it is the bigtooth maple in the high canyon lands of the West and Southwest. The Oregon maple has some syrup, and the plains Indians also used the box elder.

Native Americans first taught the French how to tap maple trees. The French then improved the methods by using European utensils of brass or copper to boil down the sap. Before the end of the 17th century the Indians were using kettles. But they, like some syrup makers of today, did not like the continuous refining to obtain a pale, sweet syrup, arguing that the darker syrup tasted better, with the flavor of the forest.

"In late February, 'Sap Moon' in the Algonquian calendar, Indian men and women set up camp in the sugar bush. In central Illinois, sugar maple thrives on the rough and somewhat steep slopes that descend to the waterways, and may dominate the forest. These thick stands of hard maple are self-seeded.

But a productive sugar grove requires human care and attention. Indians removed brush that impeded movement from tree to tree, girdled and burned out old trees, and tended replacement saplings. By piling snow around the base of producing maples, collectors could delay the bursting of the leaf buds and extend the sap season by a week or more."

From *The Maple Sugar Book*, Helen Nearing and Scott Nearing.

"In established groves, Indian women tapped trees by making horizontal gashes in the trunks three or four feet above the ground and inserting cedar 'spiles' at a downward angle, allowing the sap to drip into elm or birch bark buckets. Before the importation of kettles, they collected the sap in wooden troughs, boiled it by dropping hot stones into the sap and stirred until granulation occurred. The sugar they stored in 'mococks', sewn birch bark bags. Men cut wood, made fires for heating the stones or kettles, and hunted and fished for camp. The integration of men's and women's work, the place of sugar-making in the seasonal round marking the end of winter, and the delightful, sweet product all lent a festive air to the occasion. Children loved to pour the boiling sap on the snow to cool into chewy candy."

From *Food Products of the North American Indians*, Commissioner of Agriculture Report, 1970.

It is easy to make your own syrup if maples grow on slopes down to your house. The old way was to drill a hole and then make a spout from a hollow sumac twig, and let the sap drip into buckets. Downhill, the buckets are emptied into a large tank or cauldron. But the long outdoor hours, depth of snow, and hidden roots may make the early season's enthusiasm fade. Now, with plastic tubing, some simple plumbinglike joints, and gravity, the sap can make its way down to you on its own.

The warmer days, increase of light, and cold nights make the sap rise. The trees need to be at least twelve inches in diameter and healthy (tapping does no harm to the tree). You can put more than one tap in bigger trees. The bigger the crown of the tree (i.e., more leaves), the more sap. Whether in a sugarhouse or outdoors, the fire under the tank needs to be constant and the liquid, mostly water, must remain at the boiling point, 212F. As the water evaporates, the boiling point slowly rises. When the temperature reaches 7F above the boiling point of water, the syrup is usually considered done. A neighbor who makes syrup told me the other day that the skill involved in the process is to avoid burning the syrup as the water evaporates. If the sap is not strained and clear as it flows into the boiling receptacle, the sandy sediment at the bottom will burn just like an unstirred pot on a hot stove. Also, he said that towards the end of the season, although the sap may run well, it becomes "milky," losing some sweetness. (I tasted it from the pipe: it was sweet to me but not to him. He detected more acid, plantlike characteristics in the liquid.)

Here's what it can all boil down to:

One small tree can yield up to twenty gallons of sap throughout the season, enough for one-half gallon of syrup.

A sugarbush of more than a hundred trees, ranging from small to large, in a lower than average year, can still produce more than sixty gallons of syrup.

It's best, but not necessary, to tap on the south side of a tree.

Never drill deeper than three inches into the tree.

The hole should tilt slightly downward toward the outside of the tree, about ten degrees.

Insert one tap for every foot of diameter.

Always keep the liquid covered.

Sap was rarely boiled down in the home kitchen, as the vapor is sticky.

Hot syrup is dangerous, like molten lava.

You need 1/4 of a cord of hardwood to boil down 100 gallons of sap.

Assorted nuts. From left to right: English walnuts, butternuts, bitternut hickory nuts. Below: Black walnuts, shagbark hickory nuts, shellbark hickory nuts.

Acorns (*Quercus species*)

There are dozens of species of oak found throughout North America, divided roughly into two groups: the white oaks, whose nuts have smooth shells and sweet kernels; and the red oaks, whose nuts have woolly shells and bitter kernels. Acorns were an important food supply for Native Americans and later for the explorers and colonists. They also provide sustenance to all sorts of wildlife ranging from quail and turkeys to bears.

All acorns are good to eat, but the bitter ones have a higher tannin content. Tannin, however, is soluble in water, so shelled whole or roughly ground acorns can be soaked in water to leach it out. Today most people soak the nuts in boiling water, repeating the process with fresh water until the liquid turns clear. The nuts, high in fat and protein, are then dried, roasted, and ground finely for breads, pancakes, and puddings.

White oak acorns

Black Walnut (*Juglans nigra*)

This strong and beautiful tree, native to North America, has fast been disappearing because it is so highly prized for furniture and also very slow growing. In our field, we have planted some that we hope will be cherished by the next generation. The nuts, round with a smooth husk, ripen in September and October and fall to the ground. Wear gloves when you pick them up because the husks have a brownish dye that will take a long time to wear off your skin. If you spread the walnuts out in the sun until they are partially dried, it will be much easier to take off the husks. The shells are incredibly tough, so it takes a firm whack with a hammer to crack them, and a pick to get out all the meat. Black walnuts have a very rich flavor that gives a distinctive taste to cakes, pies, cookies, and sauces.

Native Americans used tea made from the inner bark as a laxative, and juice from the nut husks to treat ringworm and inflammation.

Above: Pecans, mockernut hickory nuts.

Butternut (*Jugleans cinerea*)

Confederate soldiers often were called "Butternuts" because their homespun clothes were dyed with the green nut husks and the inner bark of this tree. In earlier days, Colonial settlers and those on the frontiers made the same use of the butternut harvest.

The butternut can grow as tall as eighty feet, bearing oval nuts 2 to 2 1/2 inches long, with sticky husks. In addition to eating the nutmeats, Native Americans boiled the nuts to release the oil that was then skimmed off and used like butter. Oil from the nuts also was used to cure tapeworm and fungal infection. Like the black walnut, the inner bark was made into a tea used as a laxative.

Hickory (*Carya species*)

These North American trees are somewhat similar to walnuts, but have smaller fruits with husks marked by four ridges when mature. The hickories with the best edible fruit are pecan (*C. illinoensis*), shagbark hickory (*C. ovata*), big shellbark hickory (*C. laciniosa*) and mockernut hickory (*C. tomentosa*). The time to gather the nuts is in the fall as soon as they have fallen to the ground. This group of nuts was eaten by the Native Americans in great quantities, as well as by birds and animals such as raccoons, bears, and even rabbits. In the spring, sap from these trees can be collected and boiled down to make syrup.

Black walnuts

Hazelnuts

Barberry jelly and catsup being served with a haunch of venison

Common Barberry *(Berberis vulgaris)*

Most of us probably have not had the opportunity to eat anything prepared from the tart, red fruit of the barberry. However, judging from old cookbooks like Miss Leslie's successful *Directions for Cookery,* first published in 1829, it was a 19th-century favorite for jellies, conserves, and catsups. The thorny shrub grows as tall as ten feet, and bears clusters of berries in August and September. It can be found in old fields and thickets from southern Canada as far south as Missouri and Delaware.

Barberry Juice

Cook one pound of ripe barberries in one quart of water until soft.
Cool. Crush berries and drain through cheesecloth.
Sweeten to taste with honey or sugar.

Miss Leslie's Barberry Jelly

Take ripe barberries, and having stripped them from the stalks, mash them, and boil them in their juice for a quarter of an hour. Then squeeze them through a bag; allow to each pint of juice a pound of sugar; and having melted the sugar in the juice, boil them together twenty or twenty-five minutes, skimming carefully. Put it up in tumblers with tissue paper.

Common Strawberry *(Fragaria virginiana)*

The common strawberry is much like the cultivated strawberry but on a smaller scale, and is one of the widest ranging of our wild fruits, thriving everywhere except in arid areas. Early explorers recorded them as being most abundant in sunny meadows and fields. Ripe from June to August depending on the elevation and latitude, wild strawberries are small and grow in clusters close to the ground. It takes a long time to accumulate even a cup, but the intense flavor is well worth the effort.
(I noticed when in Sweden that folk out for a walk in the short summer, when finding these *fraises des bois,* had a clever way to carry them home. The strawberries were threaded on a stalk of timothy.) It is best to enjoy them fresh and plain, perhaps rolling them in a bit of confectioner's sugar or adding a little cream. However, if you have time to pick a large quantity, use them in any recipe in place of cultivated strawberries.

Common Blackberry

(*Rubus alleghaeniensis*)

Blackberries grow in old fields, hedgerows, and the sunny edges of woods in just about every region of the United States. Their arching stems feature beautiful white flowers in spring, followed by juicy black fruits in late summer. When picking I always wear denim jeans and a long-sleeved shirt to avoid being scratched by the thorny canes. My wife's grandmother said ladies used to protect their hands by wearing worn cotton or old leather dress gloves when picking blackberries and raspberries. Blackberries can be eaten plain with sugar and cream or cooked in many ways. My favorite, deep dish apple and blackberry pie, announced the end of summer in my childhood, because both fruits ripened at the same time and were freely available. The pectin in the apples held the filling together. In addition, the tender tips of the new canes that appear in spring can be peeled and sliced into salads; and the dried leaves can be used to make tea, my personal favorite substitute for the real thing. We especially like to make blackberry brandy, because when you uncork the bottle out comes the scent, as well as the taste, of summer.

Blackberry Liqueur

Pick very ripe berries and, if they have been growing in a protected, unpolluted spot, you can choose not to wash them. If you do wash them, dry in one layer on paper towels. Fill a quart canning jar with the berries, and pour in a good quality cognac or Armangnac until it reaches the top. Cover tightly with the lid and place in a dark, cool spot for three to four weeks. At the end of that time the berries will be pale, since their color and essence have leached into the cognac. Strain through a sieve, pour the liquid to the top of a glass bottle with a tight cork or other cap, and let it rest for at least a month in a cool, dark spot. The liqueur is at its best for about eight months.

Raspberries (*Rubus* species)

We have a thicket of raspberries in a clearing near our kitchen windows. When the berries are ripe and the sun beats down on them, the fragrance wafts all the way into the house. This is our signal to get out and pick quickly before birds, bears, and other animals come to partake of the feast. When the raspberries are ripe and warmed by the sun, their taste is perfect. A great many go straight into the mouths of the pickers rather than into their baskets. These wild red raspberries *(Rubus strigosus)* have almost six-foot-long reddish canes covered with many fine thorns. They spring up in disturbed soil, clearings, the edges of woods, and roads where seeds have been deposited by birds. Depending on the specifics of climate, the fruit can be picked from June to October.

In good years there has been such an abundance that my wife has made everything from vinegar and jams to tarts and liqueurs. We tend to prefer recipes in which the raspberry flavor is predominant. Two of them follow:

Raspberry Sorbet

8 cups red raspberries
4 tablespoons framboise liqueur
1 1/2 cups sugar

1. *Place the raspberries in a food processor fitted with a steel blade and puree. Press through a strainer to remove seeds.*
2. *Add framboise and sugar and stir until dissolved.*
3. *Freeze in your ice-cream maker, following the instructions.*

Yield: 2 quarts

Raspberry Liqueur

Fill a quart canning jar with freshly picked ripe raspberries for the best flavor. Add three to five black peppercorns, preferably Telicherry, 1/4 cup sugar, and fill to top with good quality vodka. Screw on a clean lid and place in a dark, cool cupboard for one month. Remove and strain liquid. The berries will be white because their color and essence will have drained into the vodka. Fill a clean glass bottle with the liquid, cap tightly with a cork or other cap, and store in a cool cupboard for one month more.
The liqueur, now ready to drink, will have a strong raspberry flavor.
In following years, you can adjust the amount of sugar to your particular taste.

Yield: 1 1/2 pints

Blueberries (*Vaccinium* species)

You will see different members of this species growing throughout the United States in acidic soil in locations ranging from swamps to mountains: some are small, low-growing shrubs, while others can reach a height of fifteen feet. Blueberries are usually found in spots where they can get a good amount of sunshine, such as open areas along the sides of roads or at the edge of woods. The fruit is light blue to blue-black in color, covered with a grayish powder, and has numerous, soft seeds. When picking, look at the top of the berries for the five-parted crown that tells you they are edible (not necessarily choice). Poisonous blue-colored berries do not have crowns. A host of wildlife lives on blueberry fruit and foliage, and many historical journals have recorded the Native Americans' extensive use of blueberries and the similar huckleberry. A traditional harvesting practice is to spread a sheet or blanket under a bush and shake the bush, causing the ripe berries to fall — much faster than picking berry by berry! There are two ways to keep blueberries for the winter: one is to dry them in the sun like the Native Americans did (or in an electric dehydrator); the other is to freeze them quickly on a tray, then pack them in plastic bags for storage.

We like the following blueberry cake warm with whipped cream for dessert or at room temperature with morning coffee.

Sabra's Blueberry Cake

3 cups blueberries
2 teaspoons cinnamon
2 cups plus 2 additional tablespoons sugar
3 cups all-purpose flour
3 teaspoons baking powder
1 teaspoon salt
1 cup canola oil
4 large eggs
1/4 cup lemon juice
1 tablespoon vanilla
Whipped cream or ice cream

1. *Preheat oven to 375°F.*
2. *Lightly oil or spray a nine-inch tube pan and set aside.*
3. *Combine blueberries, cinnamon, and two tablespoons of sugar and set aside.*
4. *Sift the flour into a large bowl, add two cups sugar, baking powder, and salt, and stir. Make a well in the center, pour in the canola oil, eggs, lemon juice, and vanilla.*
5. *Beat with a wooden spoon until well blended, and gently fold in blueberries. Spoon the batter into the pan and smooth the top.*
6. *Bake one hour or until the sides begin to pull away from the pan, the surface is golden, and a tester inserted in the center comes out clean. Check at forty-five minutes and lightly cover with foil if the top is getting too brown.*
7. *Remove pan from the oven and let stand until warm before transferring cake to a plate. Serve immediately with whipped cream or ice cream.*

Serves 8-10

One of the freshest and simplest desserts is a wild-fruit summer pudding, of which there are several versions. I make one from crustless bread fashioned into the bottom and sides of a pudding basin, then filled with gently cooked fresh blueberries, raspberries, blackberries — whatever — with lots of sugar. After sealing the top with more bread, I let it sit for a day so that the juice and fruit flavors soak throughout. Turn it out of the pudding basin and serve with concentrated extra juice, and top with fresh cream.

Plums (*Prunus* species)

The two types of plums you are most likely to encounter are the wild plum (*Prunus americana*), a small tree that grows in moist soil in the eastern half of the United States, and the beach plum (*Prunus maritima*), a low shrub that grows in sandy coastal soil from Maine to Delaware, where my wife remembers picking them as a child. The wild plum bears small, red or yellow fruit from late August through September, and the beach plum has sweet, juicy, purple fruit. Plums dry and freeze well and are favorites for jams, jellies, and pies.

Beach Plum Clafouti

1 1/2 pounds beach plums
2 tablespoons sugar
1 tablespoon flour (optional)
1/2 cup all-purpose flour
1/4 cup sugar
1/4 teaspoon salt
3 tablespoons sour cream
2 eggs
1/2 teaspoon vanilla extract
3/4 cup whole milk
2 teaspoons butter
Confectioner's sugar

1. *Preheat oven to 375°F.*
2. *Cut plums in half and remove stones. Coat the plums in the two tablespoons of sugar and also the one tablespoon of flour, if very juicy. Set aside.*
3. *In a large mixing bowl, combine flour, sugar, salt, sour cream, and eggs, and mix lightly. Add vanilla and milk and beat until blended.*
4. *Place butter in a pie plate and set in the oven for one minute to melt. Remove from oven and swirl butter to cover bottom. Pour in enough batter to coat the bottom and bake one or two minutes until firm.*
5. *Remove from oven and arrange the plums evenly over the cooked batter. Pour remaining batter on top. Bake about thirty minutes until puffed up and firm.*

Serve immediately, or later at room temperature, dusted with sifted confectioner's sugar.

Yield: 6 servings

Currants (*Ribes* species)

Currant berries — red, yellow, or black — are found in drooping clusters on shrubs of different shapes ranging from one to six feet tall. The many species — some escapees to the wild from cultivation — generally prefer cool, moist soil, and tend to grow in woods, ravines, and along streams. It may be hard to find abundant wild currant bushes because there was a large eradication program around the turn of the century when it was discovered that a fungus killing white pines needed currants to survive. If you do find them, the fresh berries, although tart, provide a wonderful, rich flavor for desserts, jams, and wines.

Wild Grapes (*Vitis* species)

The dozens of native grapes growing all across the country in temperate climates were an important food source for Native Americans as well as settlers. Vigorous trailing or tendril-climbing vines grow towards the light on the edges of woods, along stream banks, and on trees or fences. The grapes receiving the most sun generally taste best. The broad leaves are heart-shaped with saw-toothed edges, and the greenish flowers give way to fruits from amber to blue to dark purple in color and that ripen in late summer or early fall. Many species are a bit too acid to enjoy fresh, but will still turn into excellent juices, jams, pies, or wine. The leaves also are edible and can be blanched and used to wrap around meat or rice mixtures as is done in Middle Eastern cooking. Note: Use your guidebook and do not confuse grapes with Canada moonseed, which has bitter, poisonous fruit.

The finished drink after maturing, served with homemade elder flower sorbet

Common Elder (*Sambucus canadensis*)

The fragrant, white flowers of this shrub grow in flat, umbrella-like clusters. Appearing from mid-June to July, they serve as a source of champagne and wine and are often eaten in pancakes and fritters. The shrub grows in moist soil, often in thickets, and produces tiny purplish-black berries, also in clusters, which make wonderful jam. It is recommended that berries not be eaten raw.

In the past, elder flowers or bruised elder leaves were hung indoors to keep away flies. John Evelyn, in 1664, recommended that the blossoms be infused in vinegar as a salad ingredient. In Victorian times, households kept bottles of elder flower water for sunburn and to remove freckles. An infusion or tea of elder flowers has been used for skin problems and internally for colds, flu, gas, and upset stomachs.

Tommy's Elder Flower Cordial

20 elder flower heads
2 lemons, sliced
1 orange, sliced
2 pounds sugar
1 ounce white vinegar
2 pints boiling water

1. *Place all ingredients in nonreactive saucepan, and pour in boiling water.*
2. *Bring to a boil, dissolving sugar. Remove from heat, stir, and cover.*
3. *Let sit for four days, stirring once each day.*
4. *Strain through cheesecloth, funnel into glass bottles with screw tops.*
5. *Keep in the refrigerator or in a cool, dark place.*
6. *Serve one part cordial to five parts water (or to taste) over ice, with a sprig of mint.*

Yield: 2 pints

Staghorn Sumac (*Rhus typhina*)

No doubt you have often seen thickets of sumac, distinctive in winter with their rusty fruit clusters still hanging on. You may not have realized that this same fruit makes a lovely cold summer drink. The time to pick the fruit clusters is in late summer when the berries are bright red and covered with hairs, before rains have a chance to wash away their acid. Touch the ripe fruit with your finger, then press your finger to your tongue and you will detect the sharp taste of ascorbic acid — vitamin C.

One summer we made sumac "lemonade" by placing several clusters in a stainless steel bowl, crushing them gently with a potato masher, and covering them with cold water. After they sat for about twenty minutes, we removed the clusters and strained the resulting pink liquid. You have to make this to your own taste: if it seems too weak, soak more clusters in the same water and strain; if too strong, add water. Sweeten and chill before serving.

Other edible red-fruited sumacs include dwarf sumac (*R. copallina*) and smooth sumac (*R. glabra*). Note: Do not confuse these sumacs with poison sumac, which has clusters of small, white berries.

Buildings

Living here in America, immigrants from Europe remembered farmyards with buildings set around a muddy square, or in a row, one against the wall of the next. In America the availability of space and timber often resulted in collections of structures that appeared — to the European eye — to have been dropped gently from space. The whole scene bespeaks a kind of confidence, a sense of independence and openness as if to say, "We don't care what we look like." The only boundaries might be a picket fence around the farm's vegetable garden and orchard, or perhaps a fenced stock pen. In many of today's suburbs, deliberately repetitive landscaping and identical front lawns give the impression of a conforming society. A cluster of American farm buildings has the opposite effect — it exhibits a very real sense of freedom in its disposition.

The farmyard layout may seem indiscriminate at first. It is difficult to know the order in which buildings were constructed and why they were placed where they were, until an understanding of the strategy emerges. The barn, for example, is likely to have been the farthest of the working buildings from the dangerous sparks of the house chimney. The very old farms were designed along the track connecting them to the next settlement, so the entrances faced on the road on both sides.

An old barn would have its big doors facing the prevailing wind to make threshing easier. If there was a slope, the farmer might use it to provide a barn foundation and to create space for cattle stalls so that hay and feed could be driven in and dropped down from the level above. The dairy would be near the house, but the smokehouse and privy were maintained at a respectable distance.

Sometimes it takes a bit of thought and experience to decide what a particular building was designed for. If there was no barn, at least there would be a structure that once served as a wagon shed, carriage house, or a stable, and ended up a garage-cum-woodshed. Nearly every farmhouse grew lean-to additions, or ells. In the Northeast, in Maine and New Hampshire, the linear habit of Northern England took root again. Later, as farms became more organized, buildings were linked together joining the main house, little house, back house, and barn for comfort and efficiency. In most parts of the country, however, they remained quite separate, even though in some cases connected by a dogtrot or other such device. As farming changed, buildings large and small were left in place and used for another purpose or left to fall down. Nearly every old property has on it, along with the house, the foundation of another building of some kind. There was once a barn on our place, two hundred yards from our house, right on the road.

Farm buildings in America can be roughly divided into two groups, vernacular and folk. The vernacular are workaday buildings around a farm that illustrated its growth and established its size or even its decline. Most standing stables, carriage houses, cribs, sheds, barns, and other outbuildings don't show the history, roots, or culture of a particular farm family. They likely date from the mid-19th century and follow plans obtained by suppliers, or were put up by local builders with one tried-and-true style — commonplace, but well built and designed. Contemporary vernacular farm buildings are steel framed and aluminum sided, or constructed of cinder block, both standing on poured concrete. Any wood framing would likely consist of kiln-dried 2-by-4's.

The other group is what has been called folk architecture. This is truly local, using local materials and often built by the first farmers themselves with absolutely no plans, just the firmly implanted traditions and styles of the Old Country.

Whether vernacular or folk, the working structures on a farm needed a lot more ventilation than did the house: the hay barracks, corncribs, and barns to keep the contents dry; the springhouse to keep the water cool; the dairy to keep the milk and cream from spoiling. The stables, pigpens, and chicken houses needed fresh air for the health of the animals. These requirements meant that the buildings were very cold in the winter. Today they frustrate many who want to use such buildings for living and work, since their infrastructure makes insulation difficult and expensive.

The "old log cabin" was first brought to America by the Scandinavians and Germans. Both nationalities used the same nailless method, but re-created the sizes and shapes they were used to. The Scotch-Irish settlers borrowed these styles but kept the floor plans and sizes of their former stone and thatched cottages.

A sturdy **barn**, usually the first permanent building to be constructed when families moved to new land, became the heart of the farm. It was essential for survival to shelter the animals and to protect grain and food during the winter. The barn often was constructed with better timbers and other materials than was the house. The first American barns were based on the medieval European barn, which had a wide center aisle, high roof, and narrow aisles set off by supporting columns, similar to the basilica of an early Christian church. The center aisle became the barn's threshing floor, while the side aisles became space for storing hay and for animal stalls. It was then adapted by different groups of settlers to be more functional in the varying climates and landscapes of the colonies.

English settlers in New England in the 17th and 18th centuries, for example, introduced a barn with a side entry. This style and its variations can be found throughout Canada and the U.S. Constructed of wood, brick, or stone, with three bays, the English barn has the wagon door at the center of the long wall, and the threshing floor running the width — rather than the length — of the interior.

The Pennsylvania bank barn became an archetypal American barn. It was inspired by barns in mountainous Switzerland and Bavaria, where farmers built them into the slopes. In the New World they utilized the same technique, building on a stone foundation and into the side of a hill — hence the name "bank." The bottom level allowed animals and wagons easy access to the yard, and the top level provided separate space for grain storage.

Two views of a small Wyoming barn in winter.

This 1850s' English-style barn in Minnesota was built with the up-to-date features like the row of transom windows above the door. The fencing is made of local tamarack logs.

A small carriage-house barn in Salem County, New Jersey.

The roof, the most important element of the barn, determines both the interior and exterior character of the building. The covering material was first thatch, then wood, and eventually shingle. The original pitched roof is still the most common, although later it was often modified into the gambrel roof that provided extra storage needed by larger farms. Ventilating cupolas and weather vanes became two of the distinctive and useful additions to the roofs of large barns.

As standards of hygiene rose, the milking parlor was separated from the stalls. Some well-designed cow barns became obsolete when larger cows were needed to make dairying economical — the Holstein became the breed chosen for milk production. I saw a fine barn just a few years ago that had just thirty stalls. They were too short for Holsteins, whose back legs would have stood in the manure gutter. It seemed a sad end to a great building not designed to cope with current methods.

Very early on, farmers realized that domesticated cattle had lost the ability to lead the open-air life of wild animals, and needed shelter. Before there were milking parlors, a fine day meant that the cow could be milked outdoors. It also meant that the milk would be cleaner, if we consider the state of cowsheds then. Like the stable, the cowshed and calf shed were near the house, convenient to the kitchen.

Above. An old cowshed in Denmark. Many early American barns had first floors laid out like this.

Left. A brick cattle-shed barn in Holland built as the extension to a "long house"— the farmer's living quarters at one end of the structure shared the same roofline.

Previous page. In 1836, a carriage barn was added on the end of the 1750 parsonage built for the Reverend Adonijah Bidwell. Today it serves as a shed, complete with drying racks, for the 19th-century tools and implements used in the working vegetable garden that specializes in heirloom varieties.

In deep Wyoming snow the flock cannot survive without being in the farmyard.

These orphan lambs would have been farmyard-raised.

The animals needing the least housing or cover were the sheep, originally kept for their milk and mutton. Fleece was considered a bonus. As clothing for all improved in the Middle Ages, there was an increased need for wool, and the hardy sheep became a valuable animal of the hills. In both the Old World and the New, farmers worried about the flock only during lambing time, which always occurred in the harsh days of late winter and very early spring. A shelter or fold often was built onto an existing stone wall in the usually rocky, remote terrain to give protection to birthing ewes and the lonely shepherd. In the warmer lowland all the flock needed was a windbreak, and the shepherd had his cottage nearby. Even today a flock of sheep needs little shelter. Well-maintained enclosures and the watchful eyes of shepherd and dog will suffice.

Stout hog pens at a "progressive" farm in Iowa that dates from the early 20th century.

Early records show that the pig was one of the last farm animals to be enclosed. At home in the woods or munching away at the bracken avoided by all other animals, the pig required little maintenance. (The wild boar today is most often an escapee from domestication and behaves in a manner leaving no doubt that it prefers the forest and intends to stay there.) Its efficiency as a consumer then brought the pig inside its pen where it thrived on the waste from dairy and kitchen — thus becoming another animal that needed to be near the farm wife. It's easy to see why buildings began to cluster around the house.

Sparsely haired and bred for a life under protective branches, the pig did require some shade. It also needed the stoutest of shelters, since a hungry pig in its aggressive search for food could soon wreck a farmyard. Arthur Young, an 18th-century agriculturist, said, "In a large or even a middling farm, the hog is an animal of great consequence and proper places for keeping him must on no account be overlooked." He also asserted, "Nothing about a farm will make such quantities of excellent manure as hogs well-managed."

Chickens happily being given a free range in the barn. The problem is discovering where they lay their eggs.

The farmyard chicken flock, maintained to keep the family in eggs and provide meat for the dinner table, was kept to a manageable size. Chickens were easy to feed or able to fend for themselves, and there was plenty of shelter in the barn, stables, and other buildings on the farm, so that chicken coops were not an original farmyard priority. Coops, or hen houses, might be built only after other structures were in place, or when chickens or their eggs became a particular farm's product.

Handles on the posts allow the barrack roof to be raised and lowered.

Farmers looked forward to a good crop of hay each summer and would store it under any cover once the barn was full. Many seasons of overflowing barns led to the development of the hay barrack. It originated in Holland, and in turn led to the metal Dutch barn, which on today's landscape looks like an airplane hangar without walls. The original barrack, still common in the Netherlands, has a roof that can be raised or lowered for maximum cover and air circulation.

The vents for this New Jersey smokehouse are under the eaves . . .

. . . and a Tennessee tobacco smokehouse operates in the same way.

Smokehouses were extremely important because the early farmers depended on the family pig for survival through the cold winter months. This always hungry but uncomplaining beast would eat almost anything and could put on weight rapidly — dependable food if it could be preserved.

Folk discovered long ago that pork was dangerous if not well cooked. They learned that a process of slow smoking over a wood fire would prevent the meat from spoiling, as well as improve the flavor. The building used for this process, the smokehouse, was usually a small shed not far from the farmhouse. And though hanging meat above the smoke from damp green wood seems simple enough, smoking was an art. Much time and patience would have been invested in a lone pig, and the farm family did not want anything to go wrong. The butchered pig was cut into sides of bacon and hams, salted, then hung from hooks above the earthen floor where the fire burned.

The flavor imparted from smoking came from the green wood on the fire. It might be anything but pine — apple, oak, and hickory were favored. Where trees were scarce, damp corncobs were used.

Here is some advice from Pennsylvania Dutch country: "It was important that the meat did not freeze while being smoked . . . since smoke does not penetrate frozen meat. Overheating with too much fire and not enough smoke is also very damaging. Too much heat causes the meat to become soft and may cause it to fall from the hook. [There may be] so much heat that the fat melts and is forced to the outside, the meat becomes partly fried and it becomes impossible to complete the smoking process . . . it cracks in most instances and becomes moldy, resulting in rancidness and spoilage."
From *The Pennsylvania German Family Farm*
by Amos Long, Jr.

There was just enough ventilation, usually under the eaves, for smoke to escape and to enable the fire to burn slowly. This was before the days of refrigeration: "Meats may be kept in it the year round, without being very much smoked, in as much as the smoking need be only occasionally renewed, so as to keep the flies away."
From *Barns, Sheds and Outbuildings,*
Byron D. Halsted, Editor

A working crib in Sussex County, Delaware.

The unique keystone shape of the corncrib as seen from the inside.

Today's combine harvester can bag wheat on the field. The grain is then trucked directly to the mill. Before this invention, the harvest was the farmstead treasure. Some farmers kept their grain in the farmhouse loft. This was risky not only because it attracted mice and rats but also because of the danger of fire from spontaneous combustion if the grain had not been thoroughly dried. Later there were grain bins in barns and still later railroads moved the grain quickly at harvest time. In the North and East, old granaries are recognizable by the short piers that serve to raise them off the damp ground. In addition, they were built with a double thickness of boards and no windows, to keep them tight and dry.

The **corncrib** was different. It was an American building that very much needed ventilation. It got its name from "cribbing" the interleaved logs at right angles to build up a structure, with the space in between providing ventilation. The farmer made the corncrib long and narrow, with the long side facing the wind to speed the drying of the corn. The famous inwardly tapering silhouette minimizes the amount of corn at the bottom, while keeping the heavier load at the top. When the small door opens at the bottom, the ears slide neatly out. Like granaries, corncribs were raised above ground, often standing on "mushrooms" that kept out rodents.

This local corncrib was turned into a childrens' playhouse.

Chickens peck away under a granary protected by 'mushrooms.'

A local privy in splendid isolation.

After a snowfall, a path was first shoveled to the privy or the woodshed, both conveniently near the house but most likely in opposite directions. In the 19th century, such a necessary building was barely described in guides to farm and outbuilding construction. This 1858 description can't bear to mention it by name.

"There is no building which is so generally located in the wrong place, as that diminutive house to which a name is applied that expresses the absolute importance of such a retreat. It is strange that a house which everyone is ashamed to be seen to enter, should be so often paraded in one of the most conspicuous positions that could be found, so that from all back windows of the dwelling house, it is the most apparent object in view. Probably there was once thought to be a necessity for this location of the building, arising from the idea that cleanliness required it to be placed at a considerable distance in the rear of the house. . . . The first improvement that was made upon the custom to which we have alluded, was to surround the front of the edifice with blinds, or with a trellis, behind which one might conceal himself before he made his entrance. The next improvement was to build a platform on which one might walk to it in muddy weather. At length it was removed to the extreme end of the shed, and the unfortunate person who was obligated to retire to it might skulk around the shed, and allow it to be conjectured that he might have gone on some less ignoble errand. How ever much it might be suspected, there was no actual proof that he entered the temple that stood there; and a modest female after having occupied it without being seen to enter it, might on coming out return to the dwelling house with a feeling of comparative innocence."
From *The Farmers and Mechanics Practical Architect* by J.H. Hammond

You often can identify the site of an old privy — a lush apple tree or luxuriant evergreen standing as evidence of screening and enriched soil. The farm privy was not well built of stone or brick, even if other structures were, because it periodically had to be moved when the pit was emptied. Some were comfortable enough, but hardly a place for contemplation. Winter cold, summer insects, and built-in darkness saw to that. The familiar half-moon cutout on the door would provide a bit of light on the inside walls, which were usually whitewashed for purposes of hygiene and light reflection. Sometimes the family privy would be a wide two- or three-holer of various circumferences to suit different members of the family. Pungent herbs were planted around the outside, chosen more for their effectiveness against insects than for their welcome fragrance.

A late 19th-century three-holer in New Jersey.

Before indoor plumbing there were some attempts at efficiency. One arrangement, a bit more than a hole in the ground and a covered wooden seat, was the "earth closet" in which sand, lime, or ashes were very effectively applied to break down the contents of the pit. A frequent wash of lime was a good disinfectant. The Shakers designed trapdoors in the back of their outside closets and collected the chemically treated waste for fertilizer.

A stone-floored springhouse in Tennessee.

The purpose of the **springhouse**, built at the site of the fresh water source nearest the house, was to protect the purity of the family drinking water and provide a place to keep milk, butter, and other perishables. Most were built of wood, though stone or brick were best for a cool, even temperature. The floor of a good springhouse often was paved with stone and the walls whitewashed.

There is some money in old barn boards and timbers. The rustic look is very popular these days, and a Saturday morning visit to a large hardware emporium will even show you plastic versions of boards and timbers finished in barn red, complete with simulated grain. Old farm buildings are valued for their materials as well as for their history, and exposed timber is usually dry and free of rot and termites. Almost any old timber-framed building can be dismantled, starting at the top and reversing the order of the construction. If the timbers are marked, they can easily be stored for later reassembling. (My friends who save barns have six large ones stored inside one smaller one.) The decline and removal of a working building is a sad thing, and dismantling should be done only as a last resort, when there is no other means of preservation. Some who market barns piece by piece describe themselves as performing a public service. They promote the beauty of a tidied-up landscape, and see themselves as model recyclers and removers of firetraps. They usually sell to "designers" and decorators who create kitchens with a "country" look. Old farmers are wise to those who salivate over long, dusty, two-foot-wide boards and hand-made black-iron latches and hinges, but they also know that a farm is taxed on the number of buildings standing, not on their state of repair.

There are even building rustlers. A friend of mine who owns land on the New York/Vermont border discovered on a visit that the slates had been removed from a barn roof, leaving the unprotected frame ultimately to collapse. On a later visit, all the beams and posts were gone, with only sawdust left as evidence of theft.

A Vermont barn, about to move 200 miles south.

Barn posts, beams, and rafters neatly labeled and stacked.

The **root cellar** kept the family going throughout the winter. It was humid and cool, and stored food was kept below the frost line. The dirt floor and minimal ventilation maintained a constant temperature. When central heating, washing machines, bicycles, and other domestic overflow took over the old cellar, that was the end of one of its original purposes — food storage. When old farmhouses were built on rock shelves, root crops were stored in a separate cellar, usually in a slope nearby. These were mostly made of stone, with three sides built into the hill and the fourth side facing south. They were long as well as deep, with the contents held in place by the walls and separated by boards. Other root cellars were built as mounds on flatter ground, with steps leading down to the door. Anything stored was always below the frost line, of course.

Boundaries

Dry-stone walls at Pleasant Hill, Kentucky.

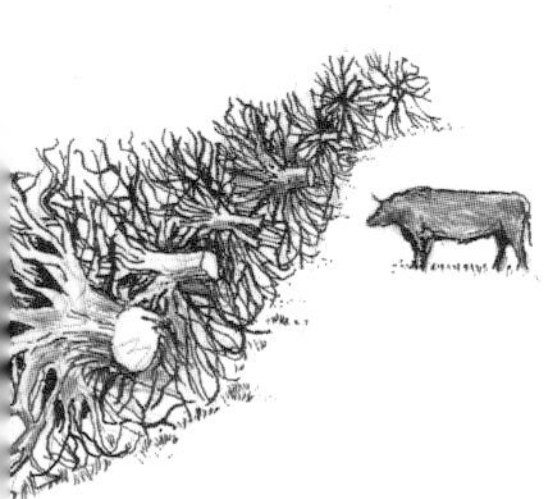

The most dramatic form of living history I have ever seen was an ancient root fence. I say "living" because those dense wood constructions take a long time to decompose — or burn. Black in the rain and bone white in the sun, these examples of concentrated energy are serious barriers, huge and hard, with their stumps as hubs. There is a measure of panic and desperation about them, like a circling of wagons, a fight against other forces of nature and the unknown. To organize the settlement of the New World, the calmer stone wall came along next, followed by the split-rail fence, the hedge, and even the sod wall when nothing else could be found.

A collapsed dry **stone wall** cannot be patched, as I have found from my own experience. One has to start all over from the ground up. The stone walls on our land, judging by trees, stumps, and old photos, were overgrown and logged out for generations. Thanks to the action of the hind feet of deer and the effectiveness of roots and brush, the discovery of our stone walls is often possible only after a light snowfall, when the silhouettes are at their best.

Although the early settlers were astonished when the right seeds took so little time to germinate and mature, they hated the stones, rocks, and boulders that had been tamped down by the primeval forest. While the farmer cursed, the patient oxen stood by, chained to the sled or stone boat they then pulled, loaded with rocks, to the planned edge of the field. There the rocks were laid, brick-like, high enough to stop a sheep or cow. As the next plot was cleared, another wall would be started parallel to the first. Any gap between the two was filled with enough earth and detritus to support the growth of a hedge. Alternately, the walls might be constructed from two parallel lines of stone built up from a wide base and filled with smaller stones and earth. Posts often were pounded into the gap to keep the more detemined rams away from the ewes; this was an adaptation

of the ancient Cornish hedge, where thorn bushes were planted in the gap. As land was cleared, even when stone walls were painstakingly laid up, an established tree would be left as a marker.

All good walls, like the Great Wall in China, are built wider at the base than at the top for increased stability. Other basic structures of architecture can be found in old walls, such as a very large stone placed across the wall — called a "through band" — that provided extra strength. If the stone was long enough, it might become a stile for the farmer.

A 'through band' in a dry-stone wall

The first stone walls in America did not have the permanence or look of labored perfection common in the Old World. The landscape was granite; the rocks were hard, but rounded and difficult to lay.

As settlers moved out and down from the glacial Northeast, limestone and sandstone were used for walls that resembled those on the British, Irish, and European landscape.

Walls were built of dry stone, without mortar. If not maintained, they would quickly give way to roots and hooves. One afternoon in Rhode Island, I saw a stone wall lose its ability to contain a flock of sheep. Spotting a dip in the wall, one ewe managed to get over it, dislodging a few stones. The flock followed, rear legs kicking backward as each one jumped, soon opening a gap six feet wide.

Walls laid by Shaker brothers in Canterbury, New Hampshire. The stones might be oddly shaped, but their facing is perfectly straight.

In heavily wooded country, settlers felled young trees and put up log **fences**. Soon after the first timber-framed houses were raised in new clearings, the trunks of young, straight trees were laid one on top of another to make simple fences. They went up in no time, their stability improved by occasional chocks. In time, thrifty farmers noticed that they could use half as much wood if they split the logs. This was the beginning of the rail fence. Up in the hills, rocks were either piled in the angle or against the rails. Evidence of this can still be found where the rails have long gone but signs of a wall remain, seemingly made by a drunkard. Snake fences were built with pride, but they took up a lot of land. At every turn in their crux a rail called a rider was laid. It was hard to knock down. My favorite was the Irish fence, never very popular but with a wonderful simplicity. Rails rest on the ground after passing through two pairs of crossed stakes.

A snake fence in the Blue Ridge Mountains.

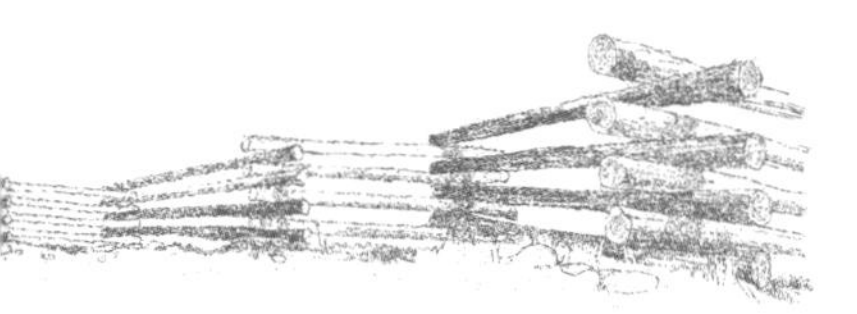

The snake, or zigzag, fence was easy to build but required the most wood — split logs or saplings — because of the need to alternate direction to maintain stability. Stone or wood placed under the bottom rails prevented ground rot.

The buck fence was used on land too uneven to build any other kind. It is named after the sawbuck, a rack with X-shaped ends on which wood is laid for sawing by hand.

The stake-and-rider fence is simple to erect. A pair of crossed stakes, often pounded a few inches into the ground, provides support. A sturdy rail, the rider, rests in the cross. The lower part is made just like a rail fence

Also easy to construct, the Irish fence consists of a series of long poles or logs: the top end is placed in the crotch of crossed stakes that are wired or nailed together. The lower end passes under the two following crosses and rests on the ground

The fences seen here serve specific purposes. Neatly sawn board fencing encloses the house and barnyard. Tighter picket fencing protects the vegetable garden. More portable stake-and-rider fencing keeps animals out of the field crops.

An Irish fence strides across the meadow.

A snake fence with stakes and riders is a style used when timber was plentiful. This one is at Old Sturbridge Village, Massachusetts.

Eventually most land was enclosed by straight post-and-rail fencing. Although they look clean and economical, post-and-rail fences take work. They need deep post holes, require effort to make mortise holes in the posts, and the split rails have to be narrowed at each end to squeeze into the hole. Early post-and-rail fence builders had to look for rot-resistant cedar, locust, tamarack, or cypress; or, as a last resort, the bottom ends of posts could be treated with tar.

The invention of **barbed wire** barely caught up with the speed of America's westward movement. It was first seen as inhumane and too flimsy. Although invented in the East, it was extensively used first in the far West, then made its presence felt by moving back eastward, changing previously hedged or fenced land.

One of the worst or best of all inventions, we are still counting the costs and benefits of barbed wire. In a society that prides itself on freedom and independence, barbed wire is a symbol of the restriction of movement and still gives an alien look to the countryside. It is the stuff that wars are made of.

Still, barbed wire was extremely effective when used in the drift fences that ran for miles east and west over cattle ranches, stopping the inclination of herds to move down to the southern areas that were easily overgrazed.

In 1874, a year after Joseph Glidden's first patent, there were still only ten miles of barbed wire fencing. Ten years later there were 250,000 miles of it. Today there are millions of miles of barbed wire fencing in the U.S. alone. The look of the existing rural landscape is clearly connected to the western world's liking for beef.

Barbed wire from a fence put up more than forty years ago.

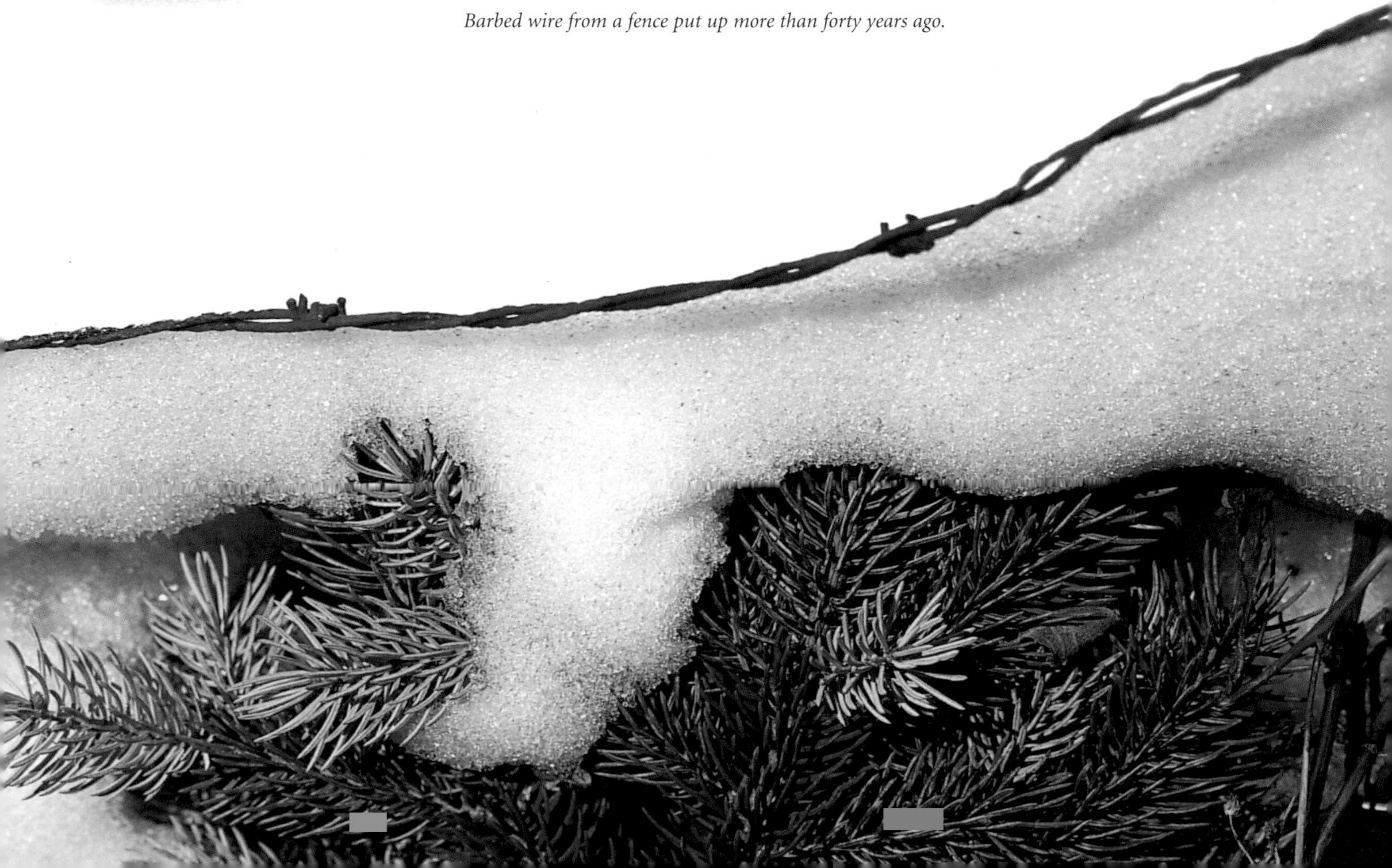

Neatly trimmed hedgerows seem to hold the land together.

Hedges, grown from seed, spread out to Missouri, to Iowa, Nebraska, South Dakota, and Oklahoma as people moved west in great numbers in the mid-1800s. The great forests of the East and North had thinned out and turned into treeless grassland except for the odd osage orange tree. A few new arrivals remembered the hedges of their homeland, wanted to encourage them, and on some wagons there was a sack full of osage orange seeds put up by enterprising sutlers in Illinois. In the desert regions, ingenious settlers made do with ocotillo cactus, which grew tall and thin and could be woven into wattlelike palisade fences. And the gulf states had the *Yucca gloriosa*, or Spanish bayonet, as an effective barrier. On the High Plains, where only grass would survive, hard work made sod fences from the very earth the plow turned over.

But America hadn't had enough time to allow hedges to grow as they did in Europe; if there had been, many of the later problems would not have occurred. In their favor, hedges were alive and they did not use valuable timber. Most importantly, they were good for the land, not just as windbreaks but in many other ways. They were the strongest stitches holding the patchwork quilt of fields together, valuable and worth re-establishing over here.

Hedges are the oldest barriers. When the Romans got to Northern Gaul and Britain they found these naturally growing but man-made barriers already in place. In our time, the soldiers after the D-Day landings found that hedges, or bocages, were a formidable obstacle for friend and foe. Established hedges have survived for hundreds of years, but in Europe have slowly but relentlessly disappeared in the name of farming efficiency.

In England, more than 115,000 miles of hedgerows have been removed in the last twelve years by developers and farmers who had invested in American equipment, designed for the prairie, that could not easily turn around on a typical European field.

Only now, after the cost has been added up, are the remaining hedgerows being left alone. They had been seen by some modern farmers as wasteful and untidy, and only needed to retain cattle in a world becoming more vegetarian. Hedges were a luxury, harbored pests, and hid precious sunlight from crops in adjacent fields; they had to be maintained and were no more than a historic feature.

An argument started when some traditional farmers and all the environmentalists wanted to keep the hedges. Earlier governments had urged farmers to grow more food crops and encouraged — even subsidized — them to remove hedges. Wildlife that had held farmland in balance began to disappear at an alarming rate. The hedges had for years helped to prevent pesticides from getting into the food chain. Aphids, a real pest for cereal growers, had been held in check by the birds and bugs nesting in the hedges. There was also a "hedge green," a permanent area left around the edge of the field so that machinery could turn. This "beetle bank," as old farmers called it, was never plowed.

Now that there is a growing public awareness of the benefits of restoring the balance of nature and retaining hedgerows, the wildlife that was almost destroyed by pesticides in the hedgeless country is coming back.

Animals

A working Clydesdale at an historic farm in England.

The **horse** was the backbone of the working farm in the 19th century, but by 1960 mechanization was almost complete. Since then there has been a small but steady increase in the number of working horses. There are several reasons for this: sentimentality, a feeling for history, and a genuine affection for the horse and the role it played in shaping the landscape. And though it seems that just about every possible farming machine has been invented, people still find tasks for a strong workhorse.

Much of the old farmland in our area has been naturally reforested, and logging is the main industry in the valleys. Ex-farmers learning about selective cutting are using Belgians and Clydesdales to harvest logs in the very hilly, often wet terrain that defies the ability of heavy, wide equipment to negotiate the narrow spaces between trees.

These big horses are descended from the Great Horse of Europe, which survived 400,000 years and four ice ages, roaming wild over the North German plains of Westphalia and the Rhineland. I remember seeing the last remaining herd several years ago, enclosed in a park near Paderborn, Germany. Their main descendants are the Belgian, Suffolk, Clydesdale, and Percheron, all originally bred as war horses to carry the weight of their own and their rider's armor, and later recruited into the work of pulling and plowing.

Today one can see these breeds at plowing contests and country fairs. Their groomed appearance and well-kept harnesses are typical — the plowman and wagoner have always taken great care of their teams and equipment.

The horse, originally hunted for meat, was so much a part of human life in France and Belgium before mechanization that it was considered a natural food source after its working days were over. During World War II the Continental Butcher Shops in every British town sold horse meat, the only meat that was not rationed. I could not bear to walk by them.

Traditions of the horse culture remain with us. Village garages and repair shops that were once smithies

A working Clydesdale at an historic farm in England.

The **horse** was the backbone of the working farm in the 19th century, but by 1960 mechanization was almost complete. Since then there has been a small but steady increase in the number of working horses. There are several reasons for this: sentimentality, a feeling for history, and a genuine affection for the horse and the role it played in shaping the landscape. And though it seems that just about every possible farming machine has been invented, people still find tasks for a strong workhorse.

Much of the old farmland in our area has been naturally reforested, and logging is the main industry in the valleys. Ex-farmers learning about selective cutting are using Belgians and Clydesdales to harvest logs in the very hilly, often wet terrain that defies the ability of heavy, wide equipment to negotiate the narrow spaces between trees.

These big horses are descended from the Great Horse of Europe, which survived 400,000 years and four ice ages, roaming wild over the North German plains of Westphalia and the Rhineland. I remember seeing the last remaining herd several years ago, enclosed in a park near Paderborn, Germany. Their main descendants are the Belgian, Suffolk, Clydesdale, and Percheron, all originally bred as war horses to carry the weight of their own and their rider's armor, and later recruited into the work of pulling and plowing.

Today one can see these breeds at plowing contests and country fairs. Their groomed appearance and well-kept harnesses are typical — the plowman and wagoner have always taken great care of their teams and equipment.

The horse, originally hunted for meat, was so much a part of human life in France and Belgium before mechanization that it was considered a natural food source after its working days were over. During World War II the Continental Butcher Shops in every British town sold horse meat, the only meat that was not rationed. I could not bear to walk by them.

Traditions of the horse culture remain with us. Village garages and repair shops that were once smithies

Animals

Sister and brother Belgians in Washington County, New York.

remain in the same family. Everyday phrases demonstrate "horse sense": "taking off" derives from the act of removing the harness; "journey" from a day of work in the field; and "set you straight," is the saying of an experienced plowman guiding a novice and a team. Even a "train" was originally a line of forty or fifty horses tethered together, panniers laden.

Among the many breeds of horses developed, my favorite (perhaps because I saw it most as a child) is the Suffolk Punch — slightly smaller than a Clydesdale, a little darker than a Belgian, and without the typical feathering of long hair just above the hoofs. These shire horses are famous for their patience, manners, and willingness to work. They are known even to go down on their knees rather than give up on a pull. They could go on longer without a feedbag than most other horses.

George Ewart Evans spoke to a number of country horsemen, plowmen, and farmers before they passed on and before their sons became tractor drivers. The men were full of stories and ready to share their tricks of horse care and training. They swore by various mixtures of herbal leaves they rubbed on, or added to the feed, to make the animal's coats shine. They were competitive amongst themselves and with other farm workers, taking great delight in the mysterious ways by which they seemed to control, or even bewitch, their horses. Taking advantage of the horse's delicate sense of smell, for example, they carried strange potions they had mixed themselves to "jade," or stop, a horse dead in its tracks. To convince the locals of his animal's loyalty, one man surreptitiously dropped a "powder" near his untethered horse to transfix it outside an inn while he had a beer or two inside.

"One cunning old horseman used to jade a horse simply by pretending to feel the horse's fetlocks, but with the palm of his hand covered with the repellent substance. Later when he wanted to release him he had only to go through the same notion but this time having his hand covered with a substance that would neutralize the smell. And he gulled, and also impressed, the bystanders by lifting up one of the horse's front hoofs, giving it two or three sharp taps with his knuckles and saying confidently: 'Right! He'll go now.'"
From *The Crooked Scythe* by George Ewart Evans

A herd of Holsteins, with one Jersey for cream.

The **COW**, bred for generations as a multipurpose animal: a source of milk, cheese, beef, traction — even burden — and eventually leather and clothing, over time has been divided into three main groups. Paintings depicted milkers, in typical farm landscapes of England and America up to the end of the 19th century, as reddish-brown-and-white shorthorn or Ayrshire cows. Today most dairy farm herds are black-and-white Holsteins, bred to produce milk in great quantities. Part of the dairy group, often just one or two in a big Holstein herd, are the small and attractive golden Jerseys, known for their very rich cream. In the West (and elsewhere) white-faced red Herefords are raised to provide most of the world's beef. The third group is made up of crossbred animals, whose characteristics are continually being refined to adapt to living or market conditions. One of these is the Brown Swiss, originally prized as a puller, then for its meat, and now for its butterfat. Another is the white Charolais from France, increasing in numbers because it matures quickly and has meat low in fat. The type of cow bred into most others is the shorthorn. Recently the strain itself has been divided into the milking and the beef shorthorn. A further development in cattle breeding has produced cows that give birth to small calves, making delivery easier and less risky. Despite such specialization, not all the early original breeds have been nudged out of the farmyard, and the cattle industry has begun to look at their virtues. In a recent test, for example, the British White, a breed dating from the Roman occupation, showed amazing potential. A young bull was randomly used in a test that compared it with animals chosen for their rapid growth rate: the best of the top beef bulls that year. The British White matched the competition for weight gain each day; and when it was examined for excess fat, it had less than any other bull in the test. Intrigued, the scientists carried out the experiment with other young British White bulls and proved that this ancient longhorn strain outperformed the modern breeds in weight gain.

Not all the old breeds can be maintained for experiments. As a result, they are under the same threat as are rare wild animals. Often, because they are not as photogenic as typical zoo animals, even petting zoos don't want them. But all is not lost. A famous zoo, in a cost-cutting move, began to feed its ancient livestock to the lions, saying that more space was needed for "wild" animals. Word got out, and Save the Tame Life groups were formed. Also, many of the growing number of "living history" farms have original breeds, and some new small farmers are finding out that small is beautiful when it comes to animals. Take the pretty Irish Dexter cow: she is half the size of a Holstein and gives half the milk — just right for today's family.

Cattle coaxing at Colonial Williamsburg.

If you stop to look at, or walk through, a herd of cows, their heads will turn toward you for a slow stare, then they'll resume grazing. Those that slowly walk toward you are probably heifers or bossies, still young and curious. They will stop when you stop, and you can gently shush them away. Sometimes there is a young bull amongst them. This is a prospect that frightens some youngsters but puts others in the mood for the excitement of the famous Running of the Bulls in Pamplona, Spain. Ferdinand usually ignores you — your red coat and all. But if he starts pawing the ground and backs away while facing you, then care is needed and the exits should be examined. The following action is not recommended but has worked. Here, the pitchfork becomes a symbolic banderilla:

"On one occasion Red Light got in with the herd of pedigree Guernsey cows . . . and there were panicky telephone calls from the family for me to go and remove him instantly. I went over armed with a pitchfork. I knew he would always try to back up to get a run at whoever was annoying him, so the only thing to do was to keep advancing on him with the pitchfork and he would keep drawing back. This he did, making nasty noises and digging holes with his feet to try to get enough room to charge, and I successfully backed him the three or four hundred yards to my own land. Colonel Miles was immensely impressed. I heard him telling his friends afterwards that I had fixed the bull with my eye and had forced him back, that it was great credit to my willpower and courage, etcetera, etcetera. In reality I was frightened out of my wits and knew perfectly well the only way to prevent him charging me was to keep walking forwards so that he would keep walking backwards."
From *Seventy Summers* by Tony Harman

Nature's lawnmowers at rest in a parklike setting.

Sheep need little care, being placid outdoor animals. But American culture, for the moment, has passed the sheep by. Once supremely economical for wool and meat, the development of artificial fibers and changes in food preferences have drastically reduced the number of sheep in this country.

The great lawns of England were cropped by sheep. Grass regularly grazed this way is as fine as any in the world, with an even, manicured texture and few weeds except for wild thyme (which gives the meat flavor if the animals are butchered). Sheep need little water except in very dry country; they seem to get enough moisture from the grass. Only slightly less difficult to control than goats, they try to act like them, always looking for an opening in a fence; and sheep can jump almost as high as goats can. A determined ram will try to butt down what he can't jump over and can swim a river to get at ewes. The biggest problem — apart from predators — for anyone thinking of having a small flock of sheep is the handling of the wool each spring. Sheep shearing is difficult, and one has to find the whereabouts of a not-too-distant professional shearer.

There used to be a saying, "She's as common as mutton." It would now be taken as a compliment, for since 1970 the U.S. total of some 20,000,000 sheep has fallen to half that number and is still falling. Many Americans have never really been fond of the taste of lamb and mutton; in some areas one has a hard time finding top-quality lamb. The combination of beef, pork, and chicken leaves lamb with about 1 percent of the market. In fact, the prospect of government-supported lamb from New Zealand spurred the U.S. government to aid threatened U.S. farmers by taxing the imported meat, thus keeping its price level with the domestic variety. New Zealand does have one advantage, however — its spring lamb is born in August and arrives in time for Christmas. In the Old World, home-grown lamb is the first choice for Sunday dinner. French restauranteurs fly their buyers to Welsh meat markets to obtain the choice carcasses of lambs raised on salt-air grassland. Like the goat, the sheep was once a chosen source for milk and cheese — Roquefort, for example.

Regrettably, this hardy, low-maintenance animal is now a rare sight in the American landscape except in some parts of the West. Thousands and thousands of miles of overgrown stone walls in the eastern U.S. attest to the existence of the extensive wool industry of yesteryear. We are lucky that there is still no substitute for tweed.

This flock of long-haired hill sheep shows the mixing of breeds — Blackface, Derby, and Cheviot.

SOME SHEEP WISDOM

Once sheep have grazed a field, the next crop planted there will be a winner.

Wether: castrated male.
Teg: ewe having her first lambs.

Save the best hay for the lambing ewes.

Wethers fatten faster than rams.

Feed sheep a large amount of parsley to prevent foot rot.

Marking paint must be of a type that doesn't downgrade the wool.

Let lambs go unclipped, 'till June be half worne,
The better the fleeces will grow to be shorne.

You may begin to shear your sheep
When elder blossoms begin to peep.

The shearing pays the shepherd.

Leap year never brings a good sheep year.

Ewes yeerly by twinning rich masters do make,
The lamb of such twinners for breeders go take.

Unlike the goat, the sheep is happy enough in the cold and rain.

Each ewe will provide one hundred pounds of meat or eight pounds of wool.

One acre of meadow will support four sheep.

Many years ago, canny farmers buried their wool when they thought the price was going down. They knew it never rotted.

All dogs, unless properly trained, will chase and do great harm to sheep, which are no match for most dogs. Electric fencing seems to be effective at keeping unwanted dogs away. At the same time, no sizeable flock is complete without its sheep dog, and to see one of these animals at work is to see country life at its finest.

Tradition says the two black piglets at the front teat will grow to be the biggest of the litter.

Most domesticated **pigs** are descended from the wild pigs of southern China or the very wild European variety. Easily the most intelligent of farm animals, they can organize themselves into family groups and build nests of clean vegetation, depositing their dung and urine elsewhere. Life in the shade has given the pig a thick skin, but it is thinly haired and sensitive to sunlight, hence the sight of a pig wallowing like a hippo in the cooling mud on very hot days. But don't let this comical image fool you; hunters have found that the wild pig is violently aggressive in defending its territory.

Throughout history the domesticated pig has saved many poor families from devastating hunger, and nearly every medieval farm painting shows at least one.

When confined, the pig needed less room than other farm animals but could also be herded into the woods to grub up acorns or root around in the undergrowth. Peasants understood that everything they fed their pig would become flesh to keep them alive through the winter. The spring piglet might weigh as much as three hundred pounds by the time it was butchered in the fall. The smoked or pickled parts would last until spring.

A pig is a lot of animal, but its disadvantages are mostly superficial. It (like the male goat) has a repellent odor. Pigs don't jump but can knock down fences and posts with ease. Pigpens should be stoutly built of brick, with concrete or cobbled floors. Any lesser structure will need constant rebuilding. Pigs can even dig themselves out of enclosures.

Pigs are the most photogenic farm animals.

The simple advantages of the pig are these: rapid growth and large litters — a sow may have twenty piglets a year. In the past, the pig worked well in the dynamics of the farmyard, eating all the farmhouse food waste and thriving on the cast-off whey from the dairy. Furthermore, there was no need for a compost heap. When let into the orchard, pigs gobbled up the windfalls, often getting slightly drunk as the fruit fermented in their stomachs. During the war, when my family experienced acute food shortages, the local government issued special lidded garbage cans in which all the edible scraps were thrown in order to feed the pigs that would then feed us.

SOME PIG WISDOM

Baby pigs are very shy.

A starved pig is worse than none at all.

Pigs fatten well on meal of barley.

Pigs killed in the wane of the moon
will have inferior meat.

Unless your bacon you would mar
Kill not your pig without the R.

The first American pigs were brought
over to the West Indies by Columbus.

A Rhode Island Red hen, just about to get the bug at the bottom right. The lettuce leaf on the left shows a near miss.

Serious gardeners don't want chickens anywhere near their vegetable rows because hens will peck away at the wrong type of green stuff; but with some common-sense fencing in the right places, non-laying hens will thrive on scattered seeds, hay, bugs, and grit, and get rid of their fleas with a nice dust bath.

The chicken farms that produced eggs and roasters for cities became an industry after World War II. In today's diet-conscious America, they have become principally a producer of white meat. (Good chefs will have nothing to do with America's factory-farmed chickens; they have their own suppliers.) There are no longer old-fashioned chicken farms; rather, there are controlled environments for the broiler industry. The supermarket chicken breast is from a well-fed, seven-week-old bird.

A controlled environment on the Delmarva Peninsula.

Eggs, unlike broilers, are no longer a growth industry. They also come from a similarly controlled environment, which in simple terms is operated by the light switch. In the country, hens lay more eggs as the days get longer because the longer day means more activity, more feeding, and therefore more eggs. So inside the plant the light stays on. It's an endless spring of fourteen-hour days of artificial sunlight.

Knowing that eggs and broilers come from the factory often inspires a collective nostalgia, and many folks have their country dream of owning a little flock of chickens. The hen that lays the best eggs will not be as tender as a non-broody one, we think, but both will taste a lot better than anything shrink-wrapped. And there is nothing like one's own *coq au vin.* (French farm people use the fresh blood to make the proper base for this delicious mixture from the farmyard, vegetable garden, and vineyard.)

But keep in mind that feeding laying chickens is not that simple — or inexpensive for that matter. A hen lays about two hundred eggs a year. She will need between-three and four ounces of good dry feed every day, and vegetables are needed in the diet as well.

Light Sussex hens getting some real sunlight.

SOME CHICKEN WISDOM

After a hen lays for two years, put her in the stewpot.

A hen should lay four eggs a week to be worth keeping.

If fed properly and kept clean, chickens will stay healthy.

When a chicken gets croup, give it leaves of rue.

Add chopped nettle leaves to chicken feed for good health.

Gather eggs once a day but be sure to leave the nest egg.

Monday is the best day to set a hen.

Never eat a hen mauled by a fox.

Burn dry herbs, juniper, or cedar to fumigate the hen house.

When a late-night visitor arrives for supper, and the poultry house is dark, grab the hen sleeping next to the cock; she is sure to be the fattest.

The chicken wire should go well into the ground. Foxes, coyotes, raccoons, opossums, and rats can burrow in, and even Rover, unless taught otherwise.

Chicken manure is the most powerful of all fertilizers. But the droppings on wood or concrete can dry like pigment on an oil painting.

"Crestfallen" comes from the time when the rooster's coxcomb droops from old age, inactivity, or threat from a younger, stronger bird.

Hens are good mothers and have frequently hatched orphan ducks and geese. As a non-swimmer she will go berserk if one of her charges heads towards the pond.

Chicken feathers make good dusters.

The bird is easier to pluck right after killing, before rigor mortis sets in, and will be tender and roast quickly.

For a week or two before killing, give poultry some barley mash mixed with skimmed milk.

The familiar white "Donald," or Long Island, duck came from China. It was the original Peking Duck.

The **duck** is a newcomer to domestication, but like the goose, it was always preferred in early America because it had more fat — and therefore better taste — than did chicken. After a duck has been roasted and the fat drained away from the meat, the flavor makes even the best chicken taste ordinary. Duck eggs are not popular because their flavor is pronounced and unpleasant to most consumers. The mass market prefers the tasteless chicken egg. Perhaps more important, the shells of duck eggs are more fragile than those of chickens and have less resistance to disease and transportation.

Ducks don't need as much shelter as do chickens and can manage without a pond unless predators are nearby. Female ducks are not very good mothers. Ducklings may follow mom everywhere because they don't trust her to be around when needed. If they are abandoned, a broody hen, if available, will look after them.

To protect his ducks from a persistent fox, a friend used a bend in the stream on his property to create an island. He then added a drawbridge, which was pulled up at night. A portable wire coop to protect newly hatched ducklings for their first few weeks was placed so that its solid end was a further deterrent.

SOME GOOSE WISDOM
Goose feathers were used for quills, and the down was gently plucked for filling pillows, a task that could take all day. If you do take on the job, keep away from any breeze and don't sneeze. The feathers will go everywhere and will take hours to settle down.

The look-alike goose and gander mate for life, as do swans. Ganders often fight amongst themselves.

Keep geese away from young trees; they will damage the bark.

One acre of grass is just about right for ten geese.

In the South, geese were let out into the cotton fields to eat the weeds. This was known as "goosing down."

Geese are easier to keep than chickens or ducks and are excellent and hardy "watchdogs." They can almost look after themselves, though a determined fox will go out of its way to seize a mother on the nest.

In the past, the goose was the original top-of-the-table bird, fit for the best occasions and, pound for pound, the most expensive. Everything about the goose was preferred: its taste, its lard, of course its liver. Its size made it just right for the whole family, even though it had nothing like the heft of today's domestic turkey.

Raising the Christmas goose gave country folk a way to anticipate a special occasion in their normally routine lives. The goose was happy through the spring and summer, fattening itself on grass. But at Michaelmas, when grass stopped growing and it had to be fed with grain, the connection with feasting began. The goose would be killed the week before Christmas and hung in preparation for its traditional roasting on Christmas Day.

Geese don't need a pond but do need a great deal of water. If allowed to wander they will turn your vegetable garden into a wasteland. They are incredibly messy; while they devour grass voraciously, their rich droppings will burn and kill their very food source.

The poor old turkey is a farmyard outcast. The domestic version is not quite sure what it is. The turkey is like a big, clumsy chicken, but needs bigger and better shelter, a more varied diet, and more extensive health care than its feathered cousins. And to top it off, like guinea fowl, they are incredibly noisy.

"They [turkeys] are amazingly stupid — from the newly hatched poults who can starve to death while trampling in their feed because they haven't learned where to find it, to the hens who lay their eggs standing up. . . . They are easily frightened. An acquaintance of mine who raised turkeys commercially went wild every Fourth of July because the fireworks in a nearby village invariably sent thousands of birds piling up in corners where they would suffocate unless he waded in and unpiled them. Airplanes going overhead had the same effect, and they didn't care much for thunder, either. And turkeys are much more susceptible to disease than other fowl are, especially if raised around chickens."
From *The Homesteader's Handbook to Raising Small Livestock* by Jerome D. Belanger

Growing Your Own

I think I'm a terrible gardener, but I'm beginning to enjoy it more. Since moving to the country I have raised our produce. I imagine my gardening has been heavily influenced by my childhood experiences in the backyard when I worked with my grandfather in his garden, or allotment, or shirked when asked to help my father or the neighbors. The British seem to enjoy the challenge of gardening: the possibility of beating the odds; growing plants in Britain from far-flung countries of a past empire; gardening in a climate that means working in the damp and drizzle.

The "temperate" British climate may, in the long run, be best of all for growing, but it's the long run that I remember more than the results. It was when I moved to upstate New York that I saw the difference. A few days after sowing, the seedlings came up with what I thought was astonishing speed. This was very encouraging. I had been used to watching and waiting, covering the plantings with cloches, praying for sun, and pulling up weeds that appeared well before the pale green dots of lettuce.

Two flowers I like—he amazing flower of the artichoke and the ug-scaring marigold.

The wisdom collected on the next few pages, learned from personal experience, is mostly for the first-time gardener and is almost entirely about food, or plants that add to its flavor. I am not interested in cultivating flowers except when they are edible. (I do like to have them around, and when our fields are ablaze with wildflowers, walking our path through them is a favorite pleasure — with no work necessary.) My wife thinks otherwise. She grows flowers with various scents and bright colors. They would look good in our fields, too. It's just flower beds I don't like. They evoke suburbia and parks with "Keep Off" signs. My wife says my view of gardening is really all about the war and survival.

Why grow vegetables, anyway? Supermarket produce is cheap, and with refrigeration and shipping as well as greenhouses and advances in plant genetics, practically independent of season. In most places there are also local farm stands and markets. It is my opinion that gardening should be the country newcomer's first activity. It's the opportunity to meet nature at the halfway point. Gardening, just like farming, can be arduous, but at least a decision as to the size of the garden can be made according to one's own capabilities.

Gardening is creative labor, and unlike factory or office work, one gets to see the product all the time. Gardening is also work that can keep us alive. Our bodies are designed for bending, digging, planting, and picking. The technology-minded Shakers, for example, knew this, and for a long time the hands of their many garden workers won against the machine.

Gardening tools are simple and have evolved over many generations. They are forgiving to use, too, and take left handed people into account more than most other gadgets. (I noticed, when I studied their gardening methods, that the gardening forks, spades, and hoes the Shakers used were longer than most others and easier on the back.)

A Shaker spade.

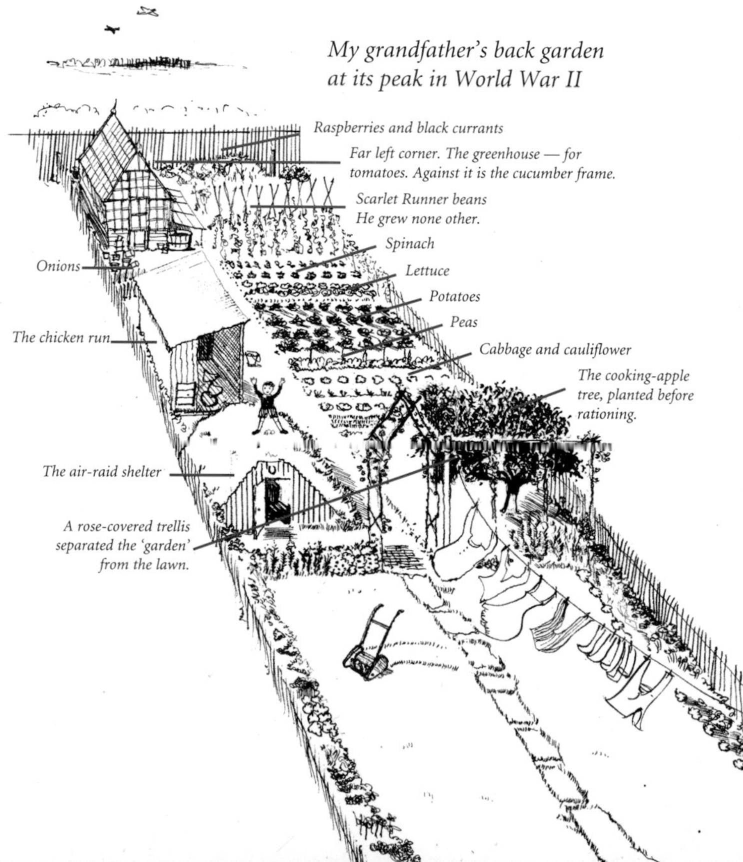

My grandfather's back garden at its peak in World War II

The vegetable **garden** is like a farm in miniature. The plot has to be plowed or dug, fertilized, weeded, and harvested in the same farming year. The beds can be seen as fields with crops that do, or don't do well next to each other. Parts to be left fallow or rotated, and conditions in surrounding planted areas, whether good or bad, will also have an effect.

Even before you start to think about the vegetable plot, it is a good idea to have something growing by the kitchen door, cherry tomatoes in pots, or herbs, for example. They will benefit from the shelter of the house and probably do better than in a more exposed site. From there you can choose the place for the garden. There is usually one good spot, and it has been used before.

Today, though, aesthetics have become increasingly important. New arrivals to the country have often moved the garden patch away, preferring a flower-edged lawn, and have paid the consequence. Tucking a garden away from sight, even when fenced, invites unwelcome visitors. The farming people where I live put their plots in the middle of a big open area near the house. This is usually effective, and there is no need for fencing. The critters, rodents, deer, and birds prefer cover — to come from, or run to when discovered — and avoid open spots instinctively. They know the distance they need to get out of trouble. An open plan makes digging, tilling, and altering the size of the garden much easier as well.

The first mistakes we all make, no matter what the packet says, are to plant and grow seeds too close together and to grow too much. I have found from experience that there is no safety in plant numbers and that reducing the number of plants by thinning will, in the end, produce a bigger and better crop. I'm still amazed at the quantities of vegetables this climate can produce compared with that of most of northern Europe. I grow squash and cucumbers near a fence because eventually I have to throw a lot of them over it.

The first garden is often a success, but it is difficult to repeat that success the following year. One reason is that the weeds that had been choked out by established grasses will return more strongly on the disturbed ground in the second year. Most first garden plots benefit from long dormancy. They are full of natural nutrients, well-balanced, and fresh to the spade. An undug meadow is less compacted, "breathes" well, and has found its equilibrium. Sir Albert Howard, the pioneer of organic gardening, saw that topsoil contained more air than its subsoil, enabling organisms to release food to plants naturally. Also, organic matter reproduces itself. Howard dedicated his life to proving that the raw material was the most important factor in organic gardening and that the way to bigger yields was to bring air and organic matter together in the soil, mixing it and making the soil lighter. He argued forcefully against tradition, insisting that artificial nitrates and phosphates were unnecessary and that nature did the job better. Today the word "organic" is everywhere, but we can ruin Sir Albert's work easily, obliterating valuable topsoil by digging too deeply and turning the airless, nearly dead subsoil to the surface.

Digging your own garden is the way to discover its secrets. Wear gardening gloves or be prepared for blisters. My first big digging experience was to earn pocket money as a ten-year-old. My task was to "turn over" a heavily overgrown 50' x 50' plot with a garden fork. I had to dig down and come up with a large, grass-covered clod, shake it, break it up, and throw the top and its roots onto a pile. I was to continue this until I had tilled the whole garden. After half an hour, palms already blistered, I had had enough. The earth seemed to be solid, wet clay, drilled with long dandelion roots, and the clods — when I could lift the fork — stuck to the tines like glue.

I was screened by a solid wall from the neighbor who was exploiting me for the equivalent of twenty-five cents, so I began to dig down and just turn over the earth, effectively covering up the surface green. The air began to dry the exposed soil. In my determination to finish the job (or to make it look like I had), I actually improved it. My customer took a look, threw some lime over it, and seemed well-pleased. He could find all the roots later. But what I did turned out fine. Organic matter had been dug into the soil. It decomposed in time for the spring planting.

Michael Pollan's *Second Nature* is the perfect book for anyone thinking about starting a garden for the first time. It is about how a garden can fit into the wild and how we can be reconciled to it (after a few battles). It is worth reading for the chapter on weeds alone. As Pollan learned, weeds are us, and the distinction between weeds and American wildflowers is yours to decide.

Most of the weeds that plagued the European gardener came to America as stowaways. Daisies, St.-John's-wort, crabgrass, clover, timothy, buttercups, Queen Anne's lace, groundsel, lamb's-quarters, chickweed, and more came over in domestic animals' manure, in the earth used as shipboard ballast, mixed in with grain, even affixed to soles of boots. Dandelions were brought over for salads, plantain roots to make flour. Even tumbleweed arrived accidentally from the Ukraine as settlers from that far country reached the High Plains. These imported seeds could wait patiently, for years if necessary, for the one thing they needed to thrive — plowed ground. I have become increasingly interested in learning which of these weeds are edible, not just dandelions for their young salad leaves and violets to accompany the peppery nasturtium flowers, but burdock, jewelweed, lamb's-quarters, sheep sorrel, and many other invaders. The more we eat them the more they'll disappear — perhaps.

So here are a few lessons I've learned about (relatively) painless gardening. First read about the soil itself, then the plants, their fruit and what can be done with them, and some gardening wisdom. Later we will all be ready for leeks, celery, and the pursuit of asparagus.

The delicate-looking yellow sorrel below usually comes up in the spots where my wife grows her salad nasturtiums. It has a nice lemon flavor.

Your garden **soil** needs a balanced diet if it is to remain — or become — healthy. Don't treat your soil like dirt. Kits available at garden stores allow you to test the amount of soil acidity or alkalinity (pH) and then adjust its composition for your growing purposes.

Topsoil is the loose layer of earth that supplies plants with the nutrition they need to grow and develop roots. In order to have soil with a good texture for growing, you need to concern yourself with its main ingredients — sand, clay, and humus.

Sand, composed of large and loose particles, makes for a light and easily worked soil but one with no food value. Soil with too much sand will dry out quickly and needs feeding with organic matter to help bind soil particles and hold water.

Clay is a tightly bound mass of tiny particles. Soil with too much clay, called "heavy" soil, holds water and obstructs the passage of air. When dried out, clay soil can become as hard as a brick. Clay, however, is chemically active and provides plant food; therefore, the ideal is to have clay and sand in proper proportion.

Humus, which is decomposed organic matter, also serves as a storehouse of the nutrients needed for successful plant growth. Thus, it is important to build up the soil's humus content. In addition to the nutrients provided, the microorganisms in decomposing humus help protect plants from diseases and insects.

Depending on varying conditions and needs, there are other substances a gardener can add to help correct imbalances or make soil richer; they include manure, compost, green manure, leaf mold, seaweed, wood ash, and lime.

Manure usually means animal dung, and the best comes from cows, horses, and pigs. Cow manure obtained from winter feeding is preferable because it does not carry the weed seeds or insect pests as does manure from pasture feeding. Horse manure is very rich because the animal's diet includes a large amount of grains high in plant nutrients. (Fresh animal manure should be composted, not applied to the garden immediately.) In addition, poultry manure is considered of great value if it is mixed into the compost heap. If getting and curing fresh manure is too difficult, bags of composted manure are available at your local plant nursery.

Three-stage compost bins.

The compost pile refers to the place where vegetable materials decay and, through the generation of heat, turn into humus. When decomposed, the material will be black-brown, slightly moist, and will bear no trace of the original grass, eggshells, vegetable peels, etc. Properly made compost actually smells sweet, like a walk in the woods.

The best way to compost organic matter into humus is to start with a good container. The optimum height is around four feet — high enough to maintain necessary heat but not so high that matter is packed down too much. A three-stage bin with removable sides makes it easy to turn the compost and also provides an ongoing supply of humus. Graded bin size allows the maturing compost to be turned into the next smaller bin as it shrinks, and a new pile to be started in the largest one.

Green manure, often called a "cover crop," is the rye, alfalfa, or clover planted after the harvest and later tilled back into the ground. This crop supplies the soil with nutritional organic material. Green manures are perfect for gardeners who cannot compost enough material for larger areas.

Leaf mold from deciduous trees is a valuable source of humus, which lightens heavy soils and helps light soils retain moisture. Leaves are shredded to help speed their breakdown and then placed in a fenced- or wired-off area until ready for spreading on the garden. Nitrogen in the form of manure or dried blood often is added to the pile because the leaves alone do not contain enough nitrogen to feed bacteria. It may take several years to get the same fine black mold found on the forest floor.

Seaweed, one of the oldest manures known, is very rich in potash, which is beneficial to the growth of potatoes, beets, and cabbage. It also is effective because it is free from weed seeds, insect eggs, and plant diseases. Small amounts can be used to "heat up" the compost pile and accelerate breakdown, especially if first soaked in hot water. Commercial extracts also are readily available to the gardener.

Wood ash from a hardwood-burning fireplace is a source of potash. It should be stored in a dry place and mixed with other fertilizers, or spread directly on the ground at least a few inches from plant stems. When rain falls, its nutrients are leached out and absorbed by the plants. (Wood ash is especially good for tomatoes and onions.)

Lime often is needed to make the garden more alkaline. This is especially true in areas where there is no naturally occurring limestone and the soil is therefore too acid for most vegetables. Ground limestone is recommended because it breaks down slowly and is available to plants over a long period. Lime should not be used at the same time as animal manure because it causes the loss of nitrogen. Adding manure in the fall and lime in the spring keeps them well apart.

This year, as I write, our vegetable garden has been very successful. We have now learned from experience that we can have an autumn crop of peas and that we should never bother with arugula until the end of summer. (Our craving for it resulted in it bolting through the spring and midsummer.) Each year there is something new in the garden, and in the case of heirlooms, something old. I do not resist the temptation to grow the easy ones, but have given up on plants that I tried to like because they were good for me, such as radicchio and chicory.

A well-designed vegetable garden with plenty of space between rows.

The Spanish conquerors brought **tomatoes** back from Peru or the lower Andes, their place of origin, to Spain in the 16th century. These tomatoes, described in writings of the time as being small — somewhat larger than a cherry — and yellow, became known as "golden apple" or *pomo d'oro.*

Many cultivars known today are derived from this same wild species. Although the tomato was soon planted in gardens in southern France, Italy, and England, it was grown primarily as an ornamental plant for almost two hundred years before its culinary use became widely accepted.

This is 'Ronclave,' *a tall-growing indoor and outdoor tomato.*

'Gardener's Delight,' *a cherry tomato from Britain. Slightly larger and more acid than the* 'Sweet 100'.

The easy-to-grow and reliable 'Sweet 100' *brings back the flavor and sweetness of yesteryear.*

The ornamental tomato, brought over to Europe as a decorative plant.

The plum tomato, developed for the consistency of its flesh, is useful for sauces. This is 'Plumito

The hardy heirloom 'Tigerella.' *Wonderful in salads.*

Two heirlooms. The smallest, 'Yellow Currant,' *resembles the original 'Pomo d'oro' brought to Europe early in the 16th century. Next to it is the* 'Cherokee Purple,' *a native from Tennessee.*

Red Robin,' *the smallest of the cherries.*

A spider feeds on a bug among our young Beefsteaks.

I use cages for small 'Gardener's Delights' *only. Big fruit bruises easily.*

Thomas Jefferson was one of the first to raise tomatoes in this country, and his writings note that they were planted extensively in Virginia by 1782. Indeed, tomato recipes are included in Mary Randolph's *The Virginia Housewife* (1824) as well as Eliza Leslie's *Directions for Home Cookery* (1828). When tomatoes became part of American cuisine, they were always eaten well cooked in catsup, sauces, soups, and side dishes, or were pickled.

Botanically the tomato is a fruit, although legally it is a vegetable in the United States. (The Supreme Court ruled in 1893 that since it was used as a vegetable it should be considered one for the purposes of trade!)

Often, on the way home from school in early autumn, I recall our gang purloining a few ripe tomatoes growing near a neighbor's fence. We would bite into them and suck out the mixture of juice and pips, chucking the rest away. We felt that the juice was where the flavor came from. In recent years I have never been able to understand recipes that command the cook to do away with my favorite part of the tomato.

Agribusiness has developed tomatoes that are basically tasteless but have tough skins and are thus suitable for shipping long distances. As a backlash to the work of big growers, there is now a movement among local farmers and private gardeners to plant heirloom varieties. Heirloom tomatoes, with their various colors, shapes, and intense flavors are rewarding to grow — even if they don't always look as pretty as those developed by the agricultural business experts. Seeds are available through gardening catalogues, and heirlooms noted there recently include: 'Cherokee,' 'White Wonder,' 'Gardener's Delight,'

The smallest and the sweetest. Clockwise, here are 'Gardener's Delight,' 'Tigerella,' 'Yellow Canary' *(two bunches),* 'Yellow Perfection,' *and mixed ornamentals.*

'Persimmon,' 'Big Rainbow,' 'Brandywine,' 'Costaluto Genovese,' 'Evergreen,' 'Green Zebra,' 'Purple San Marzano,' 'Principe Borghese,' 'Arkansas Traveler,' 'Zapotec Pleated,' 'Yellow Perfection,' 'Red Currant,' and 'Yellow Pear.'

Start your own tomatoes indoors from seeds, or buy plants at a local nursery, which generally will carry varieties that grow best in the area. Often such nurseries will be willing to start special or heirloom seeds in their greenhouses if you discuss it with them in advance. The owners of our local nursery always encourage us to try the heirloom varieties they grow, and welcome the feedback from our experience.

Tomatoes are easy to grow if they have a sunny, well-drained spot in the garden and if the soil is prepared. Dig the soil and work in compost or decomposed manure to enrich it, since tomatoes are heavy feeders. If your soil contains a large percentage of clay, add sand and peat moss to lighten its texture. Tomatoes like soil with a pH of 6 to 6.8.

Drive sturdy, five-foot stakes into the ground next to each planting hole. As the plant grows, tie the main stem to the stake with soft twine or yarn. Be sure to set out the plants after all danger of frost has passed and cover the ground with a thick mulch to keep the soil moist and inhibit weeds. Fertilize about once a month. Good growing companions for tomatoes are onions, parsley, and carrots; bad ones are the *Brassica* family, corn, and potatoes.

To keep the plants from putting too much energy into leaf growth, pinch out side shoots when they are small. These "suckers" grow between the main stem and the leaf stem.

When the vines are loaded with tomatoes (more than one can possibly eat), there are three fairly simple ways to put some away for the winter. If there is ample room in the freezer, cherry and other small tomatoes can be frozen whole on a tray and then sealed in plastic bags. Saved this way, they can be dropped straight into soups, stews, chili, etc., and have all the flavor of fresh ones. (Note: They turn mushy when thawed.) Tomatoes can be dried either by using a dehydrator or the oven. In both cases, make sure the tomatoes are ripe but not overly soft. Rinse, dry, core, then cut plum types in half or quarters, round tomatoes into thick slices. Place cut side up on drying racks and salt lightly. Follow instructions for the dehydrator, or place tomatoes in the oven at 140°F and dry until leathery. This will take from five to eight hours, depending on the oven and the thickness of the pieces. Check often near the end of the time suggested. Cool completely and store in clean, dry quart jars. If you prefer, you also can cover dried tomatoes with olive oil.

For a basic, all-purpose sauce that can be turned into soups or more complex sauces, see the recipe at right.

Easy Tomato Sauce

This recipe requires a food mill, which eliminates the time-consuming and messy task of peeling the tomatoes.

6 quarts of quartered tomatoes
6 carrots, peeled and quartered
6 garlic cloves, peeled and halved
3 cups onions, chopped
1 cup fresh basil leaves
1 cup fresh Italian parsley leaves
kosher salt to taste

1. Rinse tomatoes, cut out stems and any bad spots. Quarter, measure, and place in a large, heavy-bottomed stainless steel or enameled pot.
2. Add carrots, garlic, salt, and onions.
3. Cook over low heat. After enough juice has been released so the bottom of the pot will not burn, increase the heat and bring to a boil.
4. Add basil and parsley. Lower heat, and simmer for 2 hours, stirring occasionally. Remove from heat and cool.
5. Place a food mill, fitted with the disk with the smallest holes, over a large bowl and pass the mixture through, a little at a time. The pulp will go though, but the skin and most seeds will not.
6. Transfer sauce to pint-size plastic containers. Store in the freezer.

Yield: 6 pints

'Gold Crest,' *ready in 67 days*
'Kelvedon Sweetheart'
'Sugar Daddy'
'Miracle'
'Indian Dawn'
'Mellogold,' *ready in 82 days*
'Earlibelle,' *ready in 71 days.*
'Green Midget' *has very short cobs.*
'Eclipse'

Corn, also known as maize, is believed to have originated in Central America and the adjoining area of Mexico, where it has been cultivated for thousands of years. It sustained the cultures of the Aztecs, the Mayans, and the Incas. Corn slowly moved north and became a staple crop wherever it was planted. As we were told in our early history lessons, Indian corn saved Captain John Smith and his party from starvation in what is now Virginia. Farther north the Indians showed the Pilgrims how to plant corn in hills and fertilize it with fish.

Country gardeners like to joke about planting corn next to a fence. The night before it's time to pick those perfect, sweet ears, raccoons will climb in and have a feast. And, if the fence is too high, a few deer will show up so the raccoons can jump from their backs into the garden and throw ears over the fence for all the animals.

Sweet corn can be grown with relative ease in most parts of the country, but it is a heavy feeder and will deplete the soil unless rotated every year. Purists take it straight from the garden to a pot of boiling water, but it's almost as good to find a local grower from whom to buy corn early in the morning just after it's been picked. Corn sugar begins to convert to starch as soon as the ears are harvested, but if refrigerated and cooked the same day, the corn will still be excellent to the taste.

Today, even with supersweet corns, each batch will differ in ripeness. As a general rule, corn retains its sweetness and crispness with very little cooking. Heat speeds the conversion of sugar to starch, so the more the corn is cooked, the tougher it will be. Plunge fresh, shucked corn into boiling water for a couple of minutes. For a different, yet rich texture and taste, ears of corn with their husks on can be soaked in cold water for thirty minutes, then roasted on an outdoor grill. The ears should be placed over very low or indirect heat for about twenty minutes, and turned several times.

Corn "smut" or "devil's corn," known as *cuitlacoche* in Mexico, is a grayish black fungus that grows on ears of corn, especially during a rainy summer. This fungus, *Ustilago maydis*, has been treasured for centuries. It was the Aztecs who gave it the descriptive but unflattering name of *cuitlatl* (excrement) and *cochtli* (asleep), from the Nahuatl words. It also is known to have been eaten by the Hopi as well as the Zuni, who thought it had medicinal powers. If collected when young and tender, *cuitlacoche* is considered such a delicacy that it is called "corn truffle"; it has a wonderful earthy and smoky taste. *Cuitlacoche* has been introduced only recently in restaurants outside the Southwest as a specialty in soups, crepes, puddings, salads, and other dishes. Most corn varieties are resistant to fungi, and American farmers make an effort to control corn smut, but there are always exceptions. One may find this delight growing in one's own garden or in the field of a neighboring farmer.

An example of corn smut on some local 'Silver Queen' that I picked in August.

Cuitlacoche *Preparation*

3 tablespoons canola oil
2 tablespoons onion, finely chopped
2 garlic cloves, chopped
4 chilies poblanos; stems, veins, and seeds removed; sliced into 1/4 inch strips
6 cups cuitlacoche
kosher salt to taste

1. Remove husks and cornsilk from ears of corn and discard.
2. Cut off the fungus along with any attached corn kernels, as close to the core as possible. Chop roughly.
3. Heat oil in a frying pan. Add onion and garlic and cook until translucent.
4. Add chilies and cook for about 1 minute more.
5. Add the cuitlacoche *and salt, cover the pan, and cook over low heat for about 15 minutes, shaking the pan from time to time. The* cuitlacoche *should be tender and moist, but not soft and mushy.*

Note: If the cuitlacoche *seems dry, sprinkle a little water on it before covering. If it is too juicy, remove the lid when almost done, increase heat, and reduce the liquid.*

Yield: About 5 cups for use in recipes

A display of new potatoes photographed in early July. You can see from the size and condition of the leaves on the complete plant that its flowers have not yet formed. The young tubers are a bit small, but full of flavor. These are 'King Edward'. *To their right are* 'Arran Pilot,' *heirlooms that are drought-resistant and can stay in the ground with thin skins longer than most other white potatoes.*

The winning combination of early summer — if you can get the ingredients to ripen at the same time. Fresh peas, new potatoes, and a little spearmint for flavor are a meal in themselves. Of course, some roast lamb also would be nice.

The "white" potato— as opposed to the sweet potato — is native to the Andes, and was developed because grains would not grow at such high altitudes. It is thought to have been a food source as early as 4000 B.C., and is known to have been widely cultivated by the time of the Incas. The first Europeans to see the potato were probably Pizarro's men. One of them, Picro de Ciezo de Leon, wrote about it in his *Chronicle of Peru,* published in 1553. It is believed he brought the potato back to Spain.

The potato did not immediately become popular in Europe, where it was regarded with suspicion and thought to be poisonous. At first it was fed to livestock. Not until the end of the 18th century did it become a staple for the poor. It also took time to be accepted in the United States. Today, of course, it is one of the world's most important foods.

Potatoes are widely grown, and you can go to your local farm stand or farmer's market to get a good selection of standards. However, there is one compelling reason to take the time and effort to grow them on your own land: the pleasure of eating tiny new potatoes fresh from the ground.

They are so tender at this stage that the skin comes away with only the slightest pressure if you rub them between your thumb and forefinger, as my daughter demonstrates.

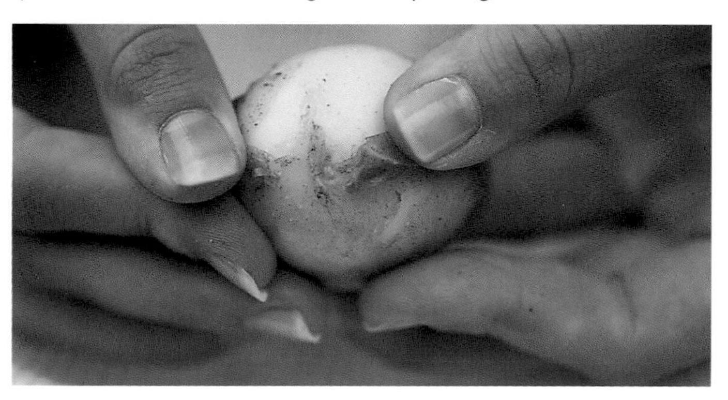

Potatoes like well-drained spots with plenty of sunshine, but are not too demanding and will do well in most soils rich in organic matter if not too alkaline. Potatoes need nitrogen, so it is helpful to prepare the ground in the previous fall by digging in decomposed manure or compost. "Seed"potatoes may be purchased from farm stores. Catalogues, however, usually offer a wider choice of the older and heirloom varieties, specially grown and treated against disease, allowing you to experience new colors, shapes, and eating qualities.

These middle-aged, or ripe, potatoes are being gently dug up in late summer.

For purposes of garden planning, note that three pounds of seed potatoes will plant one ten-foot row, fifteen square feet, or twelve hills. The best seed potatoes are small, contain one or more eyes, and do not need cutting. If cutting is necessary, leave plenty of flesh around the eyes, since plants must live on this stored food while sprouting. Two to four weeks before the last spring frost, place tubers, or pieces of tubers, about one foot apart and eight inches deep. Cover with a few inches of earth, then apply a mulch of leaves, hay, or peat to keep the soil moist and cool and the tubers from exposure to sunlight. Potatoes that are exposed to sunlight turn green and develop a toxic substance called solanin. As the plants grow, keep mulching around the stems to form a hill and make sure they receive enough water. Fertilize plants before they flower. Good garden companions for potatoes are beans, corn, cabbage, and eggplant.

Leafy vines will rise above ground and clusters of potatoes will form below. After blossoms appear, check for the new potatoes — the size of cherries — which should be ready about sixty days after planting. Dig carefully to avoid damaging the plant and tender potatoes. If you leave them alone, they will continue to grow and the skins will harden. Our favorite way to cook tiny potatoes is to boil them gently, rolling them in a little butter and adding salt. This allows their delicate flavor to come through unmasked.

This is a traditonal formal cottage garden, established before the days of Rototillers — and easy to weed.

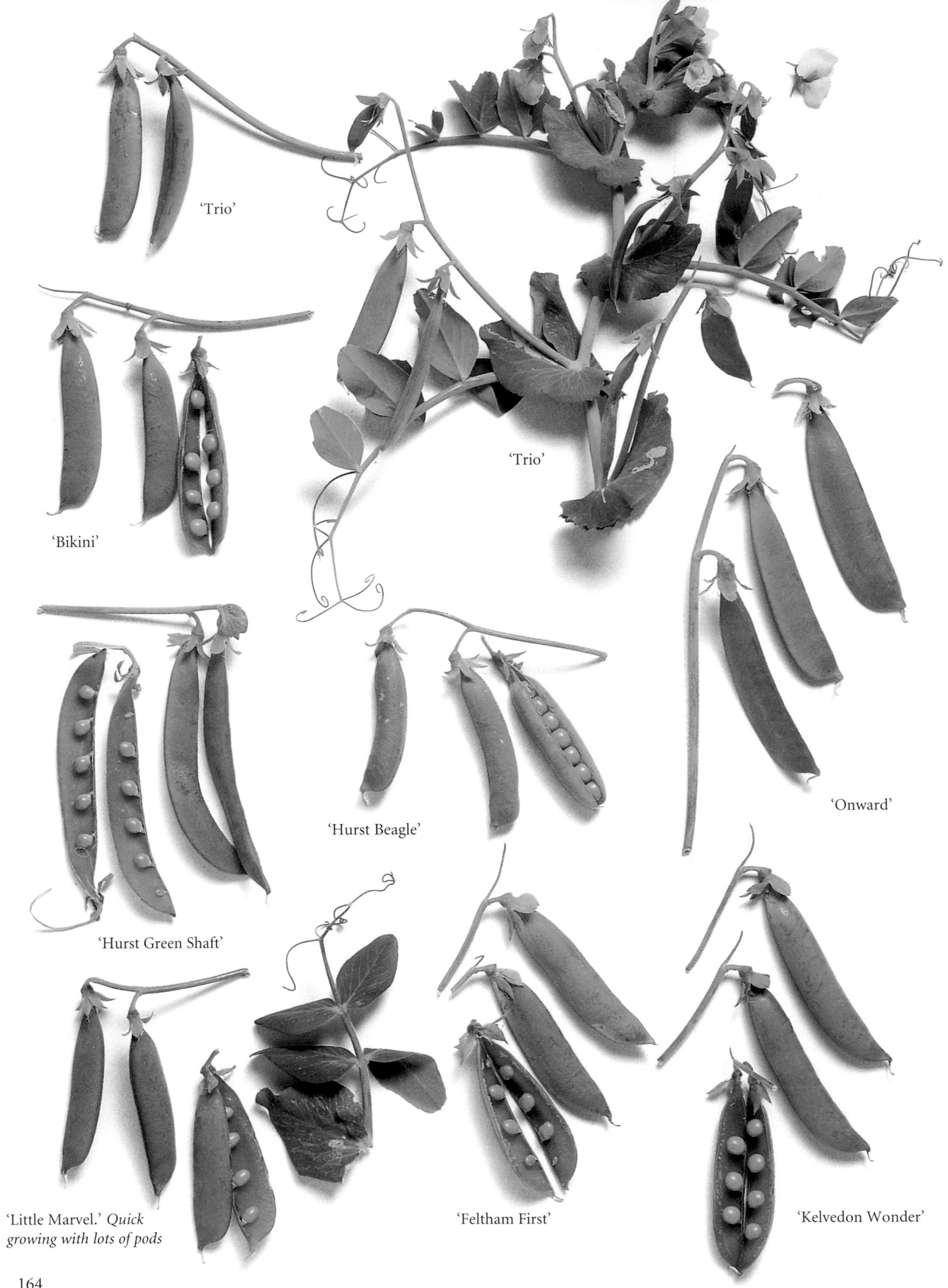

'Little Marvel.' *Quick growing with lots of pods*

Our second, late-season crop of 'Little Marvel.'

Peas are one of our most ancient crops, along with wheat and barley. Archaeologists have found peas in various Neolithic villages where people first domesticated plants and animals. Ripe peas were dried, commonly made into soup or porridge, and stored for use when other food was scarce. Some varieties of peas were also eaten fresh. By 1597, the famous English botanist Gerard recorded a type of *mangetout* — what we call snow peas or sugar snaps — with tender and edible pods.

My feeling is that we should take the time and effort to grow edibles, such as peas just off the vine, that we have a hard time getting any other way. The best way to experience the superb taste of fresh peas is to pick them yourself at the right moment and eat them as soon as possible; they are so sweet that you can enjoy both the small peas and the edible-pod varieties as raw snacks.

Peas grow well in cold weather. They can be planted as soon as the ground can be worked in the spring (but the soil must not be too wet or the seeds will rot). As soon as the plants are up, the roots need to be kept cool and moist with a heavy mulch, which also has the added benefit of keeping weeds down. In very warm regions it is best to grow peas during fall, winter, and early spring months. Peas like soil with a good amount of organic matter as well as a neutral pH, from 6.0 to 6.8. They also like phosphorus, which can be added by an application of bone meal, and potassium, which can be provided by wood ash.

There are dwarf varieties and tall climbing varieties; the latter will need support. I like the climbing varieties because the peas get more sun and will tend to escape the earth-loving slugs. Nothing fancy is needed — basic chicken wire fixed to stakes will do. Set up the stakes before planting in order not to disturb the new plants. Peas do well in the garden next to carrots, cucumbers, beans, and potatoes, but should not be planted next to onions or garlic.

Remember to pick peas young — the pods should be well filled but not yet hard — since a couple of extra days can turn sweet peas tough and starchy. Harvest edible-podded varieties when tender and just beginning to swell out with very tiny peas, or the pods will become chewy. If you have a generous crop, peas freeze easily and will be a treat months later.

Some recommended heirloom shelling peas are: 'Alderman' (tall telephone), 'Alaska,' 'Lincoln,' and 'Little Marvel.' Edible-podded peas include 'Dwarf Gray Sugar' and 'Mammoth Melting Sugar.' Check seed catalogues for others.

The **beans** grown most often in vegetable gardens today are members of the species *Phaseolus vulgaris* that originated in the Americas and were probably first cultivated thousands of years ago. Known as snap beans, common beans, kidney beans, French beans, garden beans, and filet beans, they vary in growing habits, seed and pod size, and color. Some may be dwarf, or bush, beans, while others are climbing, or pole, beans. Over the years, plantsmen have worked to produce snap beans that are "stringless" — at least when young — and therefore more pleasing to our palates. Below are some broad beans. On the right are French beans.

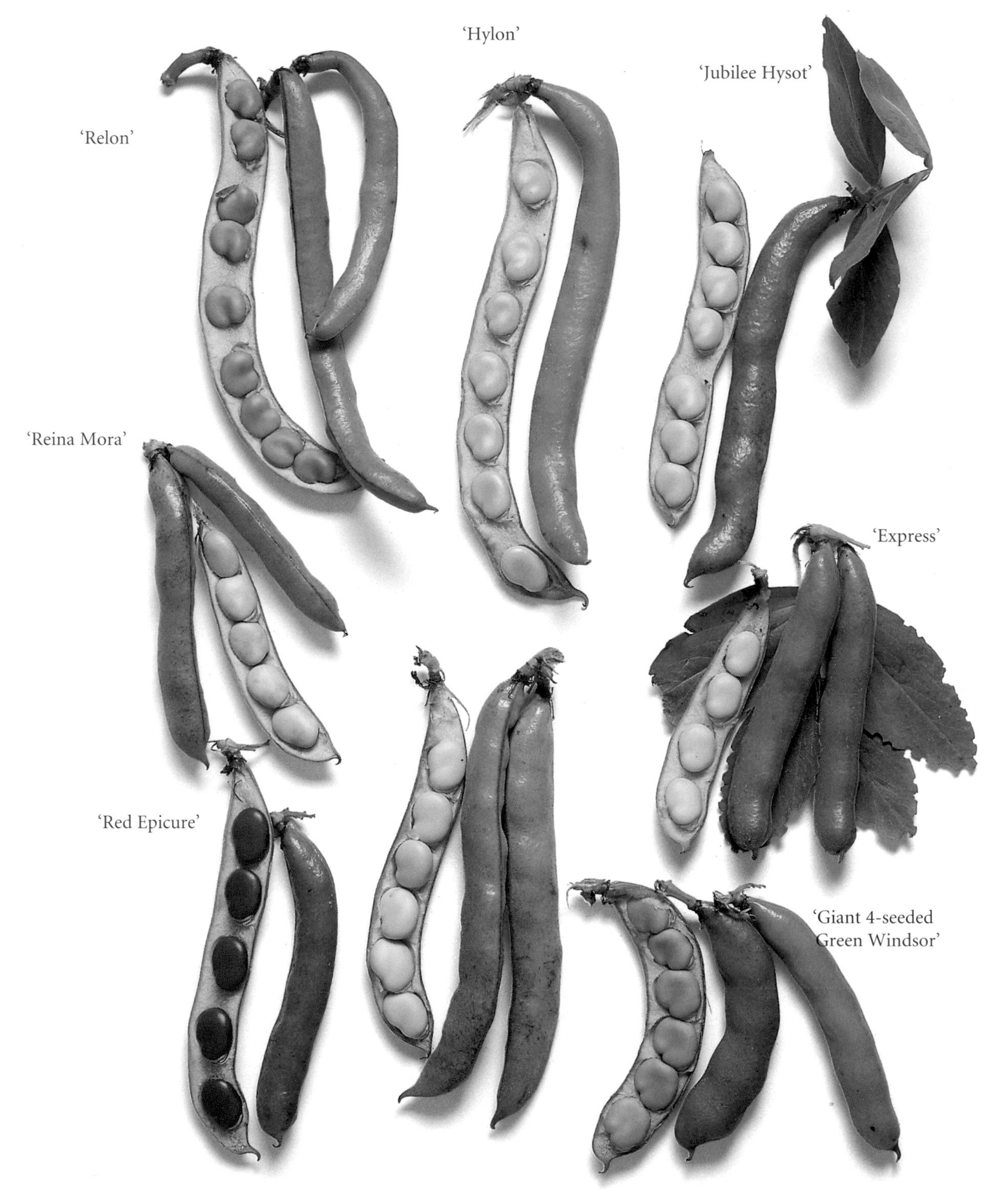

'Jumbo'
'Daisy'
'Cyrus'
'Delinel'
'Constanza'
'Loch Ness'
'Tendercrop'
sterpeice'
'Pros Gitana'
'Royal Burgundy'

Poles being made ready for 'Scarlet Runner,' *the most popular back-garden beans in Britain.*

These are our 'Scarlet Runner' *beans. The hummingbirds love them.*

I suggest adding snap beans to your garden plot not only for the pleasure of eating them when they are young and tender, but also to improve your soil. Nitrogen, a valuable plant food, is added to the soil by bacteria in nodules growing on the roots of the plants. The bacteria absorb nitrogen from the air, and the nitrogen remains to enrich the earth long after the beans are harvested. And, as gardening manuals advise, by rotating the planting of beans, new areas can be enriched every year.

Try bush beans in a sunny spot in your first gardening year, since they are the easiest beans to grow and require no support. Beans will succeed in most types of soil as long as it is not too acid and has been enriched with manure or compost. Seeds must be planted in well-drained, warm soil; they will not germinate in wet, chill weather. Don't rush to plant; wait until conditions are right. Unless you want a large supply all at once to can or freeze, plant one row at a time as seedlings begin to show above ground. A constant harvest is thus provided during the entire growing season in your area. Beans do not grow well next to the onion family, but do like carrots and cucumbers as neighbors.

Keep picking the small, tender beans so that plants will continue to produce new pods. However, don't despair if harvesting is delayed and pods grow to full size; beans can be dried for winter use. Leave the plants in the ground until the bean pods are partially dried, pull them, tie them in bunches, then hang them, roots up, in a dry, well-ventilated spot. When the pods are thoroughly dry, shell the beans and store in glass canning jars.

Among the heirloom bush beans you may want to try are: 'Black Valentine,' 'Red Valentine,' 'Tendergreen,' 'Masterpiece,' 'Canadian Wonder,' 'Bountiful,' 'Royalty Purple Pod,' 'Idaho Refugee,' and 'Black Coco.'

When driving through the countryside in the summer, one often sees wild **carrot**, or Queen Anne's lace, growing along the roads and in the fields. The English colonists brought the carrot to this country, and it is believed that wild carrots are escapees from 17th-century vegetable gardens. Carrots, first cultivated in the eastern Mediterranean area, come in shapes and sizes ranging from round to short and thin to long and thick. Although we are most familiar with sweet orange carrots, others have been developed in a variety of colors including yellow, red, white, and crimson.

Soil type dictates which carrots will grow best in your area. If you have light, loose soil you can try long, slender ones, but if you have heavy or stony soil you will be more successful with shorter varieties. The soil will need to be turned over deeply with a garden fork to loosen it. Next, work in seasoned manure or compost and remove stones. At the same time, heavy clay soils can be improved with the addition of a substantial helping of sand.

Carrots are hardy and need approximately sixty-five days to mature. The first ones can be sown early, followed by additional sowings at intervals. Make the last sowing forty to sixty days before a killing frost is expected. Soak the seeds overnight to speed germination, then drain and mix the tiny seeds with sand to help space them apart evenly. It is beneficial for carrots to grow next to chives, onions, leeks, and sage, since these plants act as repellents to the carrot rust fly, whose larvae will attack young roots. When the seedlings are up, thin carefully, spacing the strongest plants three inches apart. A bumper crop can be stored in a box of slightly moist sand in a very cool place, such as a root cellar. The green tops should be cut off and the carrots should be free of soft spots or cuts, which encourage rot.

If you are interested in sampling a bit of history, you might want to plant 'Early Scarlet Horn,' a short carrot (2 to 6 inches) developed in the early 17th century and still available. Other heirlooms of interest are: 'Touchon' (6 to 8 inches), 'Danvers Half Long' (6 to 8 inches), 'Oxheart' (5 to 6 inches), 'Belgium White' (8 to 10 inches), 'Imperator' (8 to 9 inches), 'Long Orange Improved' (11 to 12 inches), and 'Rondo' (round, 1 to 2 inches).

Queen Anne's lace and carrot flower

Lettuce was known to have been cultivated by the ancient Egyptians. Early lettuce, developed from a wild species, looked very different from lettuce today since it had a tall central stalk producing leaves. In fact, our lettuce may be remembering its origins when it bolts and sends up a seed stalk. Lettuce is thought to have come to Britain with the Romans. By the 16th century, varieties of headed lettuce were recorded. Early colonists brought seeds to this country and, of course, our famous gardener, Thomas Jefferson, grew lettuce at Monticello.

It's easy to grow many wonderful varieties of lettuce in the garden, not only all those seen in the high-priced mesclun salad bins but also those rarely seen even in green markets. The principal types are the true head, or crisphead, of which the tasteless iceberg is the most familiar; butterhead, which forms a loose head; cos, or romaine, with long oval heads; and loose-leaf, or non-heading, lettuce.

Lettuce does best in cool temperatures, so choose a planting area that receives shade, or shelter it from sun behind taller, bushier plants. If you live in an area with intense midsummer heat and a long growing season, plant in early spring and again in late summer. When you order seeds, read the descriptions carefully in order to pick the varieties best suited to your conditions. In general, loose-leaf lettuce is the most resistant to bolting

Here is properly spaced lettuce that I grew from seedlings.

from heat and takes the shortest time to mature — around forty days. Also, sow new rows every couple of weeks to provide a constant supply. A good shortcut for growing headed lettuce is to buy seedlings from your local nursery. Make certain that they've been "hardened off" — left outside for a few days to acclimate — before planting. Transplant in the late afternoon when the sun is low, then water well. These precautions will make certain that your plants experience the least amount of stress.

For the best lettuce, soil should be properly drained, rich in organic material, and not too acidic. Our garden is in an area with no natural limestone, so we need to "sweeten" the earth every season with lime in order to grow most things well. Soil can be tested with a home pH test. Moisture is essential to growing lettuce, so water regularly in dry spells. Harvest loose-leaf lettuce by picking the larger outside leaves, leaving the young center to grow new leaves. To harvest headed lettuce the entire plant must be pulled up.

Here are some of the heirloom varieties available today: Leaf: 'Black Seeded Simpson,' 'Red Oak Leaf,' 'Red Deer Tongue,' 'Bronze Arrow.' Romaine: 'Paris White Cos,' 'Rouge d'Hiver,' 'Balloon.' Butterhead: 'May King,' 'Tom Thumb,' 'Merveille des Quatre Saisons,' 'Grandpa Admires,' 'Brune d'Hiver,' 'Limestone Bibb,' 'Tennis Ball.' Head: 'Hanson,' 'Continuity Red Crisphead,' 'Reine des Glaces.'

Fall lettuce grown from seed sown in mid-August.

Squash and pumpkins,

with their trailing or climbing vines, are all members of the large genus *Cucurbita,* and as with many other plants described here, are native to the Americas. Plant historians believe that they were first cultivated for their seeds and later for their flesh. Gardeners usually think of them either as summer squash, to be eaten while their skins are tender, or winter squash and pumpkins, which remain on the vine until the rinds are hard.

'Zenith'

'Early Butternut'

The seeds you select will come from four main species. All the jokes about size and quantity, along with dozens of special cookbooks, refer to *Cucurbita Pepo*. This species includes zucchini, crookneck, pattypan, and acorn squash, and some pumpkins. *C. maxima* covers the winter squashes: 'Buttercup,' Hubbard, turban, and 'Banana,' plus the true, or "French," pumpkins. *C. moschata* includes the popular 'Butternut,' one of the winter crooknecks. *C. mixta*, grown mostly in the Southwest because of its drought tolerance, includes the 'Green-Striped Cushaw.'

'Ponca'

Gooseneck

'Sweet Dumpling'

'Delicata'

'Waltham Butt

'Clarita'
'Supremo'
'All Green Bush'
'Table Dainty'
'Burpee Golden'
'Minipak'
'Tender and True'
'Tiger Cross'

One eight-seed hill begins to expand from the garden and follows the sun onto the lawn.

Pumpkins and squash are known as "heavy feeders," so dig in plenty of compost and dried manure. Don't give in to the temptation to sow seeds too early, because they will not germinate well — or at all — in cold soil. (I must confess I've done this in my enthusiasm to get everything going in the spring.) It's better to start some seeds indoors and transplant when the soil temperature has warmed. As a beginning gardener I planted in rows, but now I make hills about ten inches high and three feet apart. Each hill gets six to eight seeds. Later I thin to the two strongest seedlings. Mulch under the vines to retain moisture, protect the fruit, and keep the weeds down.

At an earlier stage, the same planting as at top shows its potential.

Summer squash have the best taste and texture when small, but if there are some clunkers, don't feel guilty about not eating them. Just toss them on the compost heap. Take winter squash and pumpkins off the vine before frost, then cure them in the sun or in a warm, well-ventilated place for a week. If curing outside, you will need to cover them at night to protect against frost. Store in a dry place at around 55°F. And remember to add the vines to your compost heap.

There are many heirloom varieties of squash and pumpkins available. Here are a few you might want to try: Summer: 'Yellow Crookneck,' 'Cocozelle Zucchini,' 'Black Zucchini,' 'White Bush Scallop.' Winter: 'Blue Hubbard,' 'Delicata,' 'Hopi Orange,' 'Blue Banana,' 'Boston Marrow,' 'Butternut,' 'Acorn Table Queen.' Pumpkins for decoration: 'Rouge Vif d'Etampess,' 'Connecticut.' Field Pumpkins for pies: 'Small Sugar,' 'Winter Luxury,' 'Seminole,' 'White Rind Sugar.'

A friend of mine who is an expert gardener cut off a squash stalk, blew into it and made it sound like a tenor saxophone.

In Delaware, pattypan squash was sliced through like this, then dipped in flour along with little soft-shell crabs of the same size and thickness. They were then fried together in butter, making the crabs 'go further.'

When the Shakers invented the seed packet, they introduced the notion of sowing thinly. They put into each packet just enough seeds for a family plot. The instructions on the back of the packet and the handbook they produced supplied simple information without idealized imagery. Today commercial seedsmen present glossy pictures with even bigger and shinier specimens than the ones we collected and cleaned up for these pages. The truth about tastier vegetables is being told by the heirloom seed enthusiasts and the independent suppliers, in catalogues that look as though they were designed and illustrated by talented local friends who support the cause. Most importantly, these catalogues are a good read, full of opinions, anecdotes, and recipes — all of which inspire trust.

Some good-quality independent and family-owned publications

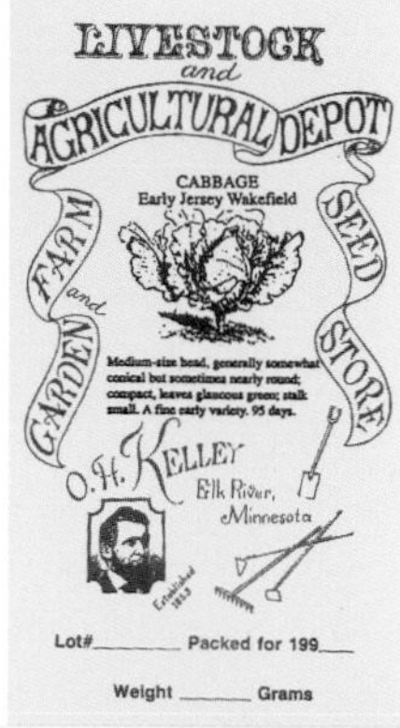

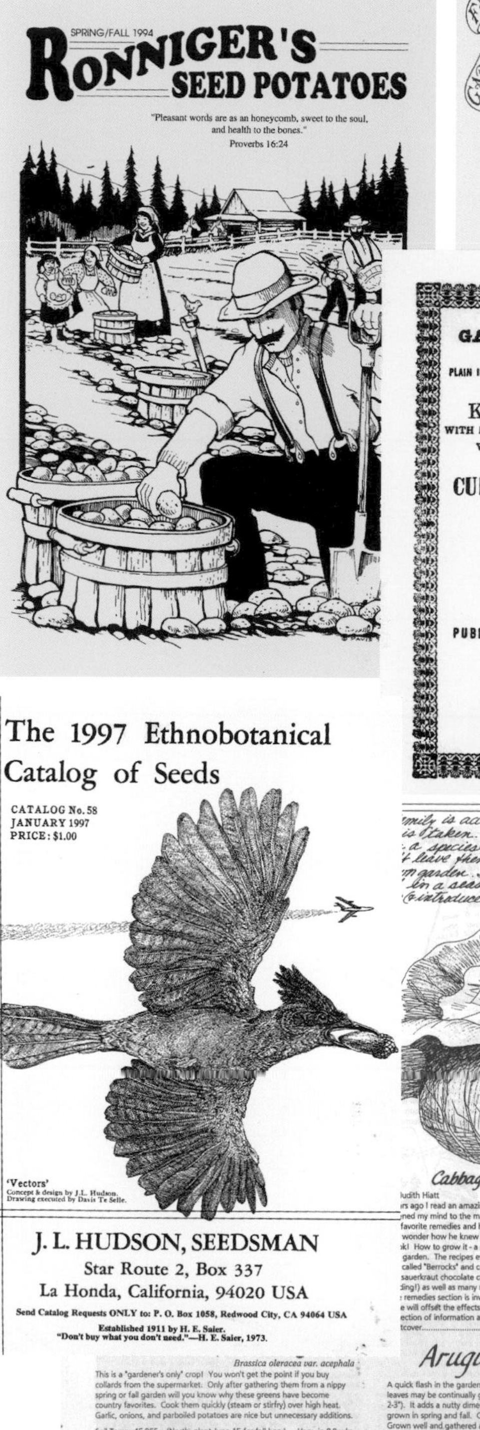

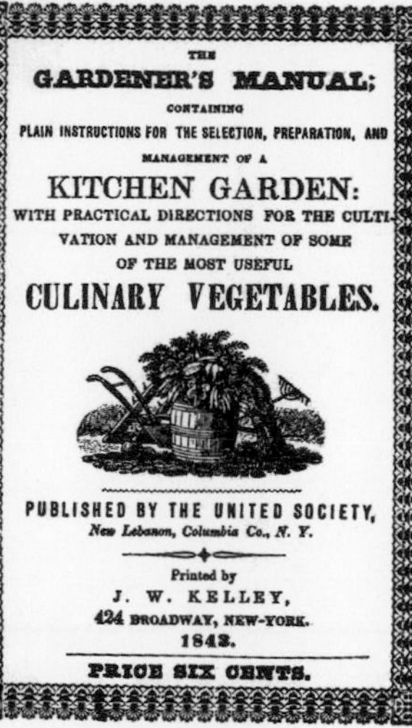

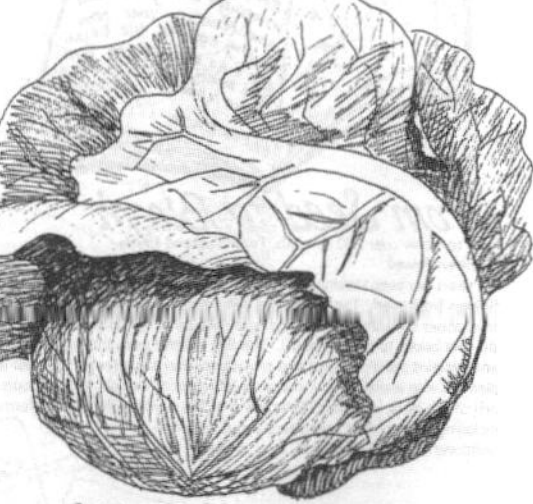

Black and white **pepper**corns, or *Piper nigrum*, were so prized for seasoning and medicinal use that, as far back as ancient Greek and Roman times and up through the Middle Ages, they were used as currency. So it is not surprising that when explorers of the New World brought back the species *Capsicum annuum*, which includes the sweet peppers and the hot pepper, it was quickly accepted and grown. Hot peppers were dried and used in place of the costly spices from the East Indies.

Sweet peppers, also called pimentos, have been a popular vegetable in kitchen gardens for years. Catalogues offer a wide variety of shapes and sizes, with tastes ranging from the very sweet — good for eating raw — to those better for frying, roasting, or stuffing. Only recently, however, have many of us also become familiar with the hot peppers used in cooking the foods of India, Thailand, Mexico, and China. We lovers of chili peppers can grow many kinds in our own gardens. Their heat depends both on the variety of pepper and on the weather — the hotter the weather, the hotter the pepper.

If your growing season is short, select early varieties — even these take about two months to mature after young plants are set out. Unless you have the right indoor conditions and are around to give regular attention, it is probably wiser to buy seedlings than to start them yourself. A local nursery may even be willing to grow from seed the special varieties you want to try. Once the soil is warm, and either in the evening or on a cloudy day, plant in a normally sunny spot, and water well. Most garden guides recommend placing a paper cup with its bottom removed around each stem to protect the young plant from cutworms. Mulch around the plants to keep the soil moist and to aid fruit formation.

Harvest peppers at any stage, but the longer they are left on the plant, the sweeter or hotter they will become. For winter cooking, we have frozen bumper crops of sweet peppers and jalapeños with great success. Here's how: Wash and dry thoroughly, then core and remove seeds and white membrane. Cut into quarters, place in plastic bags and store in the freezer. Or dice the peppers, flash-freeze on a tray for a few minutes, then pack into containers or bags for freezer storage. Mature hot peppers also can be dried: thread them on a string through the stems and hang outdoors in the dry Southwest, or elsewhere indoors in a sunny window. When dry, the pods are dark and will bend without snapping.

Here are a few of the heirloom varieties currently advertised in catalogues: Sweet: 'Nardello,' 'Figaro Sweet Italian,' 'Red & Yellow Cornos,' 'Bull Nose,' 'Cherry Sweet,' 'Golden Summit,' 'Sweet Banana,' 'World Beater,' 'Merrimack Wonder.' Hot: 'Aci Sivri,' 'Large Red Cherry Hot,' 'Ancho' (Poblano), 'Tabasco,' 'Tepin,' 'Serrano,' 'Habanero' (Scotch Bonnet), 'Thai Hot Pasilla,' 'Mulato,' 'Chili de Arbol,' 'Bulgarian Carrot,' 'Chimayo,' 'Czechoslovakian Black,' 'De Comida,' 'Long Red Cayenne,' 'Pico de Gallo.'

'Clio'

'Purple Belle'

'Gypsy'

'Hot Gold Spike'
'Cayenne'
'Serrano'
'Red Chili'

Sweet potatoes had been in a slow decline until recent years, when innovative young chefs turned their attention to American food. Many people thought of them as coming from a can, covered with sugar and marshmallows, and appearing on the Thanksgiving dinner table. They had never tasted traditional baked sweet potatoes mashed with butter and pepper, or hot sweet potato biscuits, spicy pie, or chips. Now sweet potatoes are making a comeback, and they're easy to grow if you have the right conditions.

Sweet potatoes (*Ipomoea Batatas*) — no relation to the true potato — are also native to South and Central America. They are not yams, which, if you get them at all, are expensive imports from Africa. As you might guess, they like hot weather and a long growing season, but it is possible to grow them in the North if you plant them in a sun-drenched area and cover the soil with black plastic for extra warmth. We have had successful crops at the end of a hot summer here in Zone 5 — and unsuccessful crops, too. One year our sweet potatoes, although healthy, were long and thin instead of plump. My research revealed that this result was caused by too much rain late in the season.

Buy sweet potato "slips," or rooted sprouts, from your local nursery or from a mail-order catalogue; plant after all danger of frost has passed and the soil has warmed. Push the soil along your row into ridges ten inches high (one long hill) and set the slips about one foot apart. The rows need to be three feet apart to allow room for the vines to spread. Sweet potatoes don't require a lot of extra care, but they do need regular watering until they are established.

In the North, dig sweet potatoes immediately when there are frost warnings; otherwise the plants will wilt and turn black. In warmer areas, harvest after about 120 days. Dig the tubers carefully to avoid damaging the skins, and then lay them out on newspapers to dry in a warm spot for a couple of weeks. They should be stored in a cool, dry place (55°F), layered between straw or peat moss, to be enjoyed all winter.

Sweet potatoes are either moist-fleshed with a deep orange color or dry-fleshed with a pale orange color. Some have now been developed for northern areas, with a 90- to 100-day maturity — earlier than the traditional 120-day growing period.

Sweet potato cultivars

Another tuber that originated in Peru is the 'Cassava,' *also known as* 'Tapioca,' 'Manioc,' *or* 'Manihot.' *Although I remember it from the dreadful tapioca pudding, it is a very fine source of starch. In the U.S. it is also grown as food for livestock.*

In our northern climate, **Brussels sprouts** and kale are the last two green vegetables to soldier on in the garden — hardy through frost and even snow — and we have been able to serve ours at Thanksgiving. In warmer areas, brussels sprouts are usually planted in late summer so that they can be picked from December through February. As you might guess, this vegetable was first developed in Belgium, reaching England and America in the early 1800s. The heirloom varieties are generally thought to have a much better flavor than more recently developed ones; Bedford Fillbasket is one of the traditionals you might want to try.

'Rubine'

'Bedford Fillbasket'

'Early Half Tall'

The raised beds of 17th-century gardening at Plimoth Plantation.

Some 18th-century formal vegetable plots at rest in Lancaster County, Pennsylvania.

Beans coming up in a re-created slave garden in Virginia.

Herb cutting at Plimoth.

'Albion'
'Staro'
'Kurenai Red'
'Rosso di Firenze'
'The Kelsae'

Onions always let you know when they are ready. I photographed these in mid-September. They were gathered and strung just before the first frost.

Onions and garlic belong to the genus *Allium*. If you were blindfolded, you could probably identify them by odor alone. Both have been used throughout history as medicinal remedies for everything from colds and indigestion to earaches and insect stings. Common "globe" onions have papery outer skins of various colors — white, red, brown, and red or purple — depending on the type. Onions and garlic are rewarding to harvest and keep but require a long growing season, so most gardeners plant "sets," or small bulbs, to shorten the time to maturity — about three to four months. Just don't put them next to peas or beans, whose growth they inhibit.

The look of home-grown garlic.

Cucumbers are reported to have been cultivated in India three thousand years ago, with their wild origin in the northern mountains of that country. They now come in many shapes and sizes, ranging from tiny French cornichons to those as long as eighteen inches. To grow well, cucumbers require a rich soil, warm weather, and plenty of water. And, once the plants are fruiting, all edible cucumbers must be picked so that flowering and fruiting will continue. Unless you want lots of pickles, two or three plants are more than enough for one family.

'Bush Champion'

'Telegraph Improved'
'Burpless Tasty Green'
'Kyoto'

The purple pear-shaped **eggplant** was the kind commonly seen in markets and in seed catalogues until cuisines from China, India, and Thailand became so popular in this country. Now we see many varieties, ranging from white egg-shaped and small orange to long, slender green fruits. The eggplant is believed to be a native of eastern Asia, where it was cultivated at least four thousand years ago, and to have been introduced to Europe by the Moors in Andalusia. As with several other vegetables mentioned here, the eggplant was slow to gain acceptance in Europe and the United States. The first varieties were grown more as ornamentals than as vegetables.

Eggplants, like peppers and tomatoes, belong to the nightshade family and need the same hot weather, rich soil, and long growing season — 100 to 120 days from seed. In colder areas it will be helpful to set out seedlings only after the soil is warm, and then to mulch with black plastic to hold the sun's heat in the soil.

Heirloom varieties currently available through catalogues include: 'Black Beauty,' 'Pingtung Long,' 'Rosa Bianca,' 'Thai Green,' 'Turkish Orange,' and 'Violetta di Firenze.'

'Little Fingers'

'Elondo'

'Black Prince'

'Rima'
'Slice Rite'
'Black Enorma'

Keeping the garden harvest

Root Cellars
When you grow your own vegetables it's a shame to think they must always be eaten immediately, given away, frozen, or — most ridiculous of all (and I've done it) — thrown on the compost heap. Reviving or making a root cellar to store produce out of season is a worthwhile project. Your own produce always tastes better than the supermarket versions of the same.

If you have the right conditions — a temperature between 33°F and 45°F and humidity between sixty and seventy percent — you can keep fruit and vegetables in boxes, barrels, or even heaps if they are buried in dry sand or straw. The secret is to keep everything separated. We all know how one bruised apple will affect another; before very long, rot sets in. And a root cellar can store more than just roots.

Onions, garlic, and shallots
Pull these up after the tops have fallen over, brush off excess dirt, and place in the sun for a few days to harden and dry. Then cut off the tops and place produce in mesh bags for ventilation. (Nylon mesh laundry bags are excellent and can be washed and reused.) Store in a very cool, dry area. Or, for a decorative solution, leave the tops on, braid them, and hang them in the cellar, keeping a few strands at a time in the kitchen, ready for use.

Apples and pears
These two fruits keep very well in a root cellar but need to be separated from other vegetables because they tend to absorb odors. Pick when mature but still hard and only put away perfect apples or pears, those without nicks, soft spots, or other blemishes. Let them cool overnight to lose the heat of the sun, then wrap individually in newspaper.

Place them in corrugated or wooden boxes or barrels, make a bed of hay or straw, and add hay or straw between each layer of fruit. Top off with more hay or straw. The ideal storage temperature is right at 32°F, so if you don't have a root cellar, check the temperature in an unheated basement or ordinary cellar.

Beets, carrots, potatoes, turnips
There are several effective methods for storing these root vegetables, which should be harvested in the fall when the soil is relatively dry. Brush off the dirt but do not wash. For carrots, beets, and turnips, leave the root end and about 1/2 inch at the top when cutting off the leaves. Pack between layers of lightly moist sand or peat in crates and baskets, or in corrugated cartons that have been lined with plastic bags with plenty of small air holes. Carrots and turnips (as well as leeks) also can be left in the ground and covered with a foot-deep layer of hay or straw after the ground freezes. They can be dug as needed throughout the winter. As for potatoes, dig carefully to avoid cuts and nicks, and then leave on the ground to air-dry for several hours. Put in crates or boxes and cover lightly to keep out all light. The vegetables then can be stored in a humid but well-ventilated root cellar or unheated basement maintained at a temperature between 35°F and 40°F. Leave a pail of water in the area to provide extra humidity, if necessary.

Pumpkins, Hubbard and butternut squash
Cut fruits off the vine before frost, leaving a couple of inches of stem. Let them dry in the sun for about two weeks to harden the rind, but cover at night if frost is predicted. Store in a basement, attic, or root cellar where the temperature is between 50°F and 60°F. It is best to keep individual fruits separate, in rows, rather than in a big heap.

In the South, the harvest was sometimes dried. Hanging on the kitchen wall are carefully sliced beans, tomatoes, peppers, apples, squash, and pumpkins.

There's a moment in high summer when, along with the garden vegetables, all the fruit seems to ripen at the same time. Then the wasps arrive to circle over the unpicked berries. Unfortunately, there is a limit to what one can pick and eat on the same day. The answer is to freeze — which works well for raspberries and blueberries — or make jam.

If ever I dies
an' yo ain't certain I's dead,
Just butter some biscuit
an' new made bread

An' spread 'em all over
with raspberry jam,
Then step mighty softly
to whar I am

An' move dem vittles
above my head,—
If my mouf don't open,
I'm certainly I dead.

— Monroe Sprowl

I know from personal experience that it is hard to stop birds from attacking raspberries. My friend has built a wire-roofed-and-walled cage for his canes.

Strawberries

We love strawberries but have never felt the need to grow them ourselves. Wonderful tiny wild ones — *fraises de bois* — with an intense flavor grow all across our big field. Also there are local farmers who cultivate strawberries as a specialty crop — picking them as they ripen. At their stands you can buy quarts; or for big projects like jam and freezing, you can pick berries right from the field at a very reasonable price, especially if you bring your own basket.

Raspberries

Somewhere on your property, it is quite likely that you will find a neglected patch of red raspberries that can be brought back to full production with pruning and care.

If not, think about planting canes and establishing a patch. Plants need minimum care: a well-drained sunny spot, slightly acidic soil, a bit of fertilizer, pruning, and a few nets to protect ripe fruit from the birds. We found raspberries on a sunny slope in the field nearest our house and their scent fills the air on hot summer days. In a good year, when the weather cooperates, there are so many raspberries that we not only have them for breakfast and dinner, but also make jam, raspberry vinegar, and raspberry liqueur. Then we quickly freeze extras in single layers on baking sheets and place them in bags to store for winter pies, muffins, and pancakes.

A large handful of rosemary, purple and green basil, sage, Italian parsley, and thyme. They were chopped and added (with a little cream) to our chanterelles.

Herbs

Basil

This annual with bright green leaves is probably today's most popular herb. We associate hot summer days with its fragrance, and many summer recipes call for fresh basil. Fortunately, basil grows quickly from seed and does well as long as it has plenty of sun. Seeds can be sown directly in the garden as soon as the soil is warm, and a midsummer sowing will give you small plants that can be potted and brought indoors for winter use. Basil succumbs to the first frost, so it's a good idea to make pesto for the freezer and to dry leaves in the microwave early in the summer.

Chervil
Pale green, lacy leaves top the small annual chervil. One of the French traditional *fines herbes* (tarragon, parsley, chives), it has a delicate taste a bit reminiscent of tarragon and is best when used fresh. Chervil can be started from seed and successive sowings will provide a continuous supply. The leaves may be frozen in small packets.

Chives
The most delicate member of the onion family is also a hardy perennial. In June, the long thin leaves are topped with edible purple-pink flowers that add a strong, peppery flavor to salads. The chives should be cut back at this time for a second crop. We have a long border in the vegetable garden providing chives to freeze, cut flowers for the house, and good compost material. Chives also grow well in pots that you can keep close to the kitchen door.

Coriander
The coriander plant is an aromatic annual whose fresh leaves and later seeds are used extensively in Indian, Chinese, and Mexican cooking. The seed, which has been used since ancient times, is an important ingredient in curry powders and spice mixtures, and also flavors breads, cakes, puddings, and other desserts. We sow several times directly into the garden for a good crop of leaves because the plant tends to bolt quickly. Leaves can be frozen on a tray and then stored in bags in the freezer.

Dill
This annual with feathery, blue-green leaves can grow as tall as three to four feet, and also will produce seeds. To have plenty of dill leaves for summer recipes and pickling, successive sowings in a sunny spot are recommended. The leaves can be dried in the microwave. Seeds should be allowed to ripen on the plant and then brought indoors for final drying.

Lovage
Although not so well-known in America, lovage is a wonderfully tall perennial — growing six to eight feet — that was popular in early Greek and Roman times and was always included in medieval monastery gardens. The young, dark green leaves with a celery-like flavor can be used in soups, stews, pastas, and salads. The leaves can be either dried or frozen.

Mint
There are many varieties of this extremely fragrant perennial. The mint outside our back door is spearmint (*Mentha spicata*), the one most commonly used for cooking. Mint grows so easily that it often becomes invasive, but we have not had that problem here in the North and especially love having mint to cook with new peas and potatoes. It needs plenty of moisture and quickly depletes the soil, so it is good to dress it with compost and bone meal. Mint freezes and dries well.

The herb garden at Ballymaloe House, County Cork, Ireland, famous for its home-grown and home-cooked fare.

Parsley
Italian parsley, with its large, flat, segmented leaves, is preferred to curly varieties for culinary purposes. The leaves freeze well in plastic containers or bags to be used as needed. The seeds take a very long time to germinate, so we always get a head start by buying plants at the nursery. Plants may be potted and brought inside for the winter, but keep them away from heat and give them some sunlight every day.

Rosemary
This pungent perennial shrub with glossy green leaves can live for years with the proper attention; it must be brought inside for the winter in cold climates. Rosemary thrives in full sun and is excellent with roasts, soups, stews, and vegetables; the plant is easily propagated from cuttings.

Common Sage
This aromatic bush with smoky gray-green leaves on woody stems becomes more and more handsome with age. It seems to have an affinity for chicken, duck, and pork, and is the traditional stuffing herb. Easy to grow, sage likes ordinary, dryish soil and plenty of sun. Its stems should be cut back every spring and the leaves harvested for drying in early summer before flower spikes appear.

Rocket, or Arugula
Arugula, or rocket, is an annual, native to the Mediterranean and eastern Asia. The strong and peppery leaves are best picked young for use raw in salads and pastas. Arugula also makes a great pesto on its own or combined with parsley or basil — and it freezes well. Arugula tends to bolt in hot weather, so that periodic sowing throughout the growing season is recommended for a plentiful supply.

Savory, Summer
Aromatic with a slightly peppery taste, this annual is often called the bean herb because of the character it lends to dishes whose base is peas, beans, or lentils. It germinates quickly when sown directly into the garden, and likes rich, light soil and plenty of sun. It dries well for winter use.

Sorrel, French
This perennial shoots up bright green leaves in our garden in the early spring. They are shield-shaped, with a lovely lemony flavor that adds tang to soups as well as sauces for meats, fish, and salads. Keep cutting back the leaves and the plants will send up new shoots all summer, as long as it is not too dry. If there is a plentiful crop, we remove the stems, cook the leaves for a few minutes in butter, then puree and freeze for sauces later.

Flat Parsley

Coriander

Curled Parsley

Tarragon, French

Different from other herbs because it does not set viable seed, French tarragon must be obtained as a plant. Further plants can be grown from cutting or by root division. It needs good drainage, likes full sun and good soil, but is hardy and can stand low winter temperatures. Tarragon is the important ingredient in tarragon vinegar, Bearnaise sauce, and many chicken, meat, and fish dishes. It keeps its strength when dried.

Thyme

There is almost no stew, soup, or ragout that does not call for a quantity of thyme. This low, spreading perennial has an ancient history as a medicinal and culinary herb, and bees are also very fond of its flowers. It is best to cut thyme for drying just before the buds appear, as the flavor is stronger then.

The Saffron Crocus

The saffron crocus grows from underground corms. Narrow leaves appear in summer, then lovely flowers in September with stigmas that hang out between the petals like orange tongues. These frail threads are dried to make colorful dyes and the well-known perfumed spice. Saffron is expensive because it takes many thousands of flowers to provide just one pound. It is possible to grow a number of plants and dry small amounts for yourself, but do a bit of research and buy the correct species.

Rocket, or Arugula

French sorrel

Wild sorrel

Large-leaved sorrel

Rows of freshly cut hay waiting for the binder.

Haymaking, before harvest, is the first real summer activity that concerns the country community. After all, the farm animals have to be fed later in the year when they can't forage for themselves.

The weather is usually very active in midsummer when the tall grass is ready for mowing, and the cutting and baling of hay must be done before the rain spoils it. Often all the family, friends, and neighbors pitch in during the brief windows of opportunity between showers. Fresh and green hay will keep its nutrients if dry, but if baled damp, hay will rot and be useless.

I remember that when my wife and I were visiting friends in County Clare in early summer we were put to work with everyone else. As the mown hay was gathered into bales, we had to pile these into stacks to create the smallest target for the inevitable Irish rain. That day happened to be the longest of the year, with blue skies, a breeze and enough light for us to work until eleven p.m. So rare was this occasion, and so valuable the crop, that we even had time to get most of it under cover in the stone barn before dark. At suppertime we watched television and the big news of the day featured stories from all over Ireland about tractors overheating from the

A local contractor cuts hay for friends of mine.

uncommonly long hours on the job. We were glad to have been part of an event that was happening all over the country that day. I remember, too, that haymaking may be more frantic than wheat harvesting, but it was easier and lighter work. In the old days, lifting sheaves of wheat and stacking them into stooks was hard and heavy for a youngster. The stalks were sharp and slippery, and my young arms wrapped around them could barely retain the load before it slipped down and out of control. No wonder the harvesters celebrated when all was gathered in.

Looking like big Tootsie Rolls wearing plastic raincoats, round bales of hay have taken over from the smaller, square bales in many places. Even uncovered, they present a small surface to the rain and can remain in the open for a long time.

The grower's weather

Not surprisingly, old weather lore, rhymes, and sayings deal either with the needs of mariners or farmers. What is surprising is that the odd line or two we remember (picked up even by Shakespeare) were already in the language of country folk and in verses written for their use. Here are a few — both old and new — beginning with the wind:

If New Year's Eve night the wind blowth south,
It betokeneth warmth and growth;
If West, much milk and fish in the sea;
If North, much cold and storms there will be;
If East, the trees will bear much fruit;
If North-east, flee it, man and brute.

Though winds do rage, as winds were wood,
And cause spring tides to raise great flood,
And lofty ships leave anchor in mud,
Bereaving many of life, and of blood;
Yet true it is, as cow chews cud,
And trees, at spring, do yield forth bud,
Except wind stands, as never it stood,
It is an ill wind turns none to good.

North winds send hail, South winds bring rain,
East winds we bewail, West winds blow amain:
North-east is too cold, South-east not too warm,
North-west is too bold, South-west doth no harm.

The North is a noyer to grass of all suits,
the East a destroyer to herb and all fruits;
The South, with his showers, refresheth the corn,
the West, to all flowers, may not be forborne.

The West, as a father, all goodness doth bring,
the East, a forbearer no manner of thing;
The South, as unkind, draweth sickness too near,
the North, as a friend, maketh all again clear.

With temperate wind, we be blessed of God,
with tempest we find, we are beat with his rod:
All power, we know, to remain in his hand,
how ever wind blow, by sea or by land.

The Properties of Winds by Thomas Tusser

Snow is beneficial to the ground in winter, as it prevents its freezing to so great a depth as it otherwise would.
It guards the winter grain and other vegetables in a considerable degree from the violence of sudden frosts and from piercing and drying winds. The later snow lies on the ground in spring, the more advantage do grasses and other plants receive from it. Where a bank of snow has lain very late, the grass will sprout, and look green earlier, than in parts of the same field which were sooner bare.

From *The New England Farmer* by Samuel Deane

If you can sit on the earth with your trousers down and it feels all right, then sow your barley and it will be up in three nights.

Sow corn when the moon is waxing, never when it is waning.

A damp, warm March will bring much harm to the farm.

If the blackberry comes into flower in early June, then an early harvest can be expected soon.

January blossoms fill no man's cellar.

A January spring is good for nothing.

A foot deep of rain
Will kill hay and grain;
But three feet of snow
Will make them grow mo.'

A dry May and a rainy June
Puts the farmer's pipe in tune.

If apples bloom in March,
In vain for 'em you'll sarch;
If apples bloom in April,
Why then they'll be plentiful;
If apples bloom in May,
You may eat 'em night and day.

A good deal of rain on Easter Day,
Gives a crop of grass but little good hay.

About the seasons of the year;
Astrologers may make a fuss:
But this I know, that Spring is here
When I cut asparagus.

Concerning dates, whate'er they pen
No matter whether true or not
I know it must be Summer when
Green peas are in the Pot.

And Autumn takes his turn to reign
I know as sure as I'm a sinner
When leaves are scattered o'er the plain
And grapes are eaten after dinner.

Winter is known by frost and snow,
To all the little girls and boys;
But it's enough for me to know,
I get no greens except savoys.

From *Poor Robin's Almanac*, 1808

Moving to the Country

Shortly after I arrived in America, my wife took me on a drive through the countryside of New England. We followed the valleys and hills roughly northward to the end of the Appalachian chain, which runs through western Connecticut, the Berkshire hills of Massachusetts, the Green Mountains of Vermont, and then descends from the New Hampshire mountains into Quebec. Two hours out of Manhattan, when I asked her where the country would start, she said we were already there. It was a pleasant enough ride, often by a river and mostly edged by trees, but I had expected the buildings to gradually dwindle in number and some real space to appear. I was learning the difference between the Old World and the New: Americans prefer to live right on the road, with the space behind their houses. It's a graphic example of a population on the move. Rural Europeans have spent generations moving away from the original track. Their homes are surrounded by trees, and behind walls—and if there's ivy climbing up those walls, so much the better.

A side axe like this was in constant use as land was cleared. After a tree was felled the ax was swung one-handed along the log to make a square post or beam.

The first North American settlers followed the old way. After leaving their coastal stockades, they picked sites that offered the best shelter and a degree of privacy that these independent folk felt they had earned. And they had earned it by using the most important thing they had with them—the axe. Settlers would chop a clearing in the thick forest and erect a fence to stop their livestock from wandering off into the dark green that went on forever. Their buildings were erected with the same tool and the same timber. Although mindful of their space, neighbors always helped one another, starting a tradition of house- and barn-raising that continued as people moved west.

They worked their land roughly in European field patterns. Hedgelike fences were made by rolling together the tough circling roots of the felled trees, and walls were built with stones that emerged everywhere in the disturbed ground. They tried to leave enough trees behind for future use and to hold together the fragile crust of earth resting on glacial rock. They searched for new valleys—bottom land with silt and richer soil—pushing westward towards and through the Appalachians.

When one crosses this range today, things begin to look different. Part of the reason for this is that Thomas Jefferson liked grids. His survey of 1785 started a development that subsequently divided all new United States land into square sections. With such latitude and longitude, straight roads would ease communication and be fair to all new settlers. No longer would city fathers and big landowners, with centralized power emanating from hand-picked sites, dictate the shape of things. Jefferson even dreamt of new towns laid out in grids, furthering the ideals of agrarian equality.

I must confess I don't like the look of the result, only truly visible from the air. To me, it resembles a large piece of bad modern art—thinly painted squares and circles within squares with some rubbing out here and there, unable to completely obscure the subtle original picture underneath.

The benefits and problems of this pattern are here for us to see today. Efficiency of management, harvest, and transportation led to the invention of machinery that only had to go straight, get bigger, and do everything. However, the directions of rivers and streams did not conform to the newly determined shape; some folks got water and floods, others got easily tillable earth, then dust.

Only when this plan ran up against the Rockies later in the 19th century did Americans begin to think about preservation, and then mostly in terms of scenery. Back East, people like Henry David Thoreau, and later, in the West, John Muir, began earnestly to propound the necessity for conservation.

People who move to the country today will live on land that, for the most part, has been experimented on only once. With some knowledge of what went on in their fields, farmhouses, and villages they can adapt to the combination of a new environment and existing history.

Instead of being seen as boundaries, American roads go through farms, exactly as the farmer hoped. The road was a lifeline, a sign of progress. It eased dispatch and delivery, shown by the ramp (just visible behind the first tree on the right), and allowed the folks at home on the left a safe distance from a sometimes muddy farmyard. Of all the outbuildings, the barn, the most important, was usually the farthest from the house and the sparks that might come from the house's chimney.

Traditions and Materials

When rural America pushed west, the look of communities changed in subtle ways. Immigrants from different parts of Europe brought with them not only their culture, which would hold them together while they coped with the pre-existing English, French, and Spanish, but also their special language of architecture. Ethnic islands were created on the settlement landscape, and on those islands evidence today shows house and barn shapes, orientations, and architectural details from the Old World.

Houses tend to get smaller the farther they are built from town. Except for large estates, Victorian-, Edwardian-, and Queen Anne-style porches and verandahs tend to be in village or small-town settings. In the mid-1800s, the idea of home as *villa* became popular, and all over rural America plain houses had their appearances changed by decorative elements ordered from catalogues and delivered by railroad car. Eventually, nearly all farm buildings were available this way. Many structures that were shipped by rail are fine historic buildings today.

A sympathetic view of the human impact on the countryside is best explained by wonderful examples of the vernacular language of architecture. Local materials—often just lying around for the taking—are combined with deeply felt traditions borrowed from the past.

The rich farmland of Norfolk and Suffolk yields a continuous harvest of cobbles. It's likely that the stones covering this Victorian cottage were gathered by children who were paid by the owner to fill buckets of cobbles before setting off to school on a spring morning. If one of them was lucky enough to find a stone with a hole all the way through, it would have been pocketed. This was known as a "hag stone," and was believed to be a safeguard against witches. (More on that later.) Common, too, were houses, churches, and walls faced in cobbles that had been split, revealing a flat inside surface that shone like glass.

In Michigan, the same type of round, glacial stones surfaced frequently. Here, larger cobbles are laid from cornerstone to cornerstone in neat rows, first in one direction and then the other. This herringbone pattern, as well as being attractive, actually distributes the weight more evenly. What a prosperous looking farmhouse this is, with its separate chimneys and lovely triangular attic window. It was the pride of Dr. Ticknow, a gentleman farmer and U.S. Navy surgeon, when it was built in 1844.

These sketches show the evolution of a basic American farmhouse. Of course, there are many variations throughout the country, affected by the origin of the settlers, local materials, and other influences. Shown here is what these buildings would have in common.

The early farmhouse is little more than a hovel; first one room, then two, with a mud and timber chimney. The windows are openings, boarded up for warmth. Later, leaded windows with small, diamond-shaped panes were added.

Using the same plan, a timber frame would be raised. Now the house has four rooms, a steep stairway, and a stone or brick center chimney. The doorway and windows are framed, and weatherboarding clads the exterior.

As more room was required, the now-familiar saltbox design evolved.

In the Piedmont and farther west, there is first one structure and then two under one roof. A second floor would be added later. Unlike those in the Northeast, the stone chimneys here are built outside the walls.

This is a dramatic architectural example of a prosperous farm. Ebenezer Wells built a grand addition to his home thirty years after he settled in the heart of New England.

The house at the back was typical of 17th-century dwellings, with its random placement of doors and windows, unpainted exterior, small casement windows, and stone foundation. The building's proportions show a sound construction, which meant safety and comfort to its inhabitants. The new house is a model of symmetry and style, from its brick foundation to its large windows to its clapboards painted robin's-egg blue.

These buildings illustrate the changes that took place on the land over a century and a half. As people such as farmer Wells went about their day-to-day business, America changed, in the words of Captain John Smith, from "a plain wilderness as God first made it," into a successful young nation.

A mid-19th-century view of how the farmhouse would have looked.

In the Northeast, the basic American farmhouse begins to take shape. With this longer form, there is now room for a front hall and complete separation of the downstairs rooms. A kitchen ell is added, as is a connecting workshop to the barn and other buildings.

In the Hudson Valley, the Dutch used the same form, but topped their houses with gambrel roofs. The downstairs windows are larger, and have solid shutters. The chimneys are built inside the frame and there are small attic windows. In Pennsylvania, the gable ends, combined with the chimneys, might be of stone.

Later, a porch would be added and new chimneys built for upstairs fireplaces .

Finishing Touches.
Now well into the 19th century, dormer windows appear on the raised seam metal roof. Shutters are added to the large-paned windows. Gingerbread shapes, available from catalogues, adorn the porch and eaves. The chimneys become narrower because the flues for the new, cleaner, iron stoves took up less room.

The outbuildings of Stratford Hall, Virginia

The advantages of stone buildings are their great durability; their seldom wanting repairs; their greater security against fire; and their offering to the owners places of abode of greater comfort, both in cold and hot weather. . . It may be thought by many that to erect such a one would be a great undertaking, yet it may be done without either great expense nor much difficulty. Hammered or chisseled stone is adapted to public buildings, or the houses of the wealthy, and is expensive; but comfortable, decent houses may be built with common stone, such as we would use for good field walls. Their happy owners may live freed of that continual intercourse with the paint pot, the lumber yard, and the cut nails of all sizes and dimensions. A stone house substantially put up, will last three hundred years, and will require little or no repairs for the first fifty years.

From *The New England Farmer*
by J.M. Gourgas, January 1828

These stone dwellings last forever, and need few or no repairs, so that money is well invested in them. Their quality does not deteriorate with time, like that of brick or wooden buildings.

From *Our Farm of Two Acres*
by Harriet Martineau, 1865

Next to Ireland, no other country gave up more of its population to the young United States than Norway. In the middle of the 19th century, most Norwegian immigrants went to Wisconsin. This farmhouse was built almost exactly as it would have been "back home." It is simply built, with logs selected for straightness and squared with a broad axe. A good builder could walk along a log and chop a line so straight (see example) that he would not need to go over it again with an adze. Logs were fitted together so neatly that there would be little need to fill in the chinks between them. Another source of pride was the ability to carry on a Norwegian tradition by neatly dovetailing the corners.

The beam cantilevered above the porch not only shows its construction and how the weight was distributed but also shows some prescient wisdom. As the family grew, the right corner was walled in. The near corner would eventually be walled in the same way. And, like most American farmhouses, a porch would be added later. Of all the folk who made a new life in America, perhaps the Norwegians have kept their heritage most intact. The historian Franklin C. Scott wrote: "The Norwegian-Americans have been fortunate in that they have retained a profound love for the fjords and fields of the North while at the same time they have remained conscious of the fact that it was northern nature and economic conditions that impelled them to migrate. They loved their ancestral home in Norway, they took pride in their ancient heritage. Yet they recognized in America the chance for a better life and they appreciated that too."

Near the bottom of our hollow, in the side of a south-facing woody hill, a neighbor is building a very interesting house. After acquiring the land, he set about thinning the trees, sawing the trunks into even lengths that would fit on the andirons of most fireplaces and stacking them to season. Many months later he began, by himself, to build a circular stovewood home. The beauty of this construction is that the fenestration lets in light and solar warmth as the earth moves around the sun. The form is an ancient one, with a chimney in the center for radiation, but with new ideas as well. Following the circular pattern, the logs are laid with their cut ends facing outward. The house is made with a mixture of ash, maple, and oak, trees all found in the hollow.

It's big enough inside so that straight pieces of furniture won't bump against the curved walls. And, by planning ahead, some of the logs project inside or out for storage and other purposes.

Right

A round building avoids the tricky problem of dealing with corners. However, a clever Polish immigrant farmer in Wisconsin stacked squared-off logs at the corners just as a stonemason would. The stovewood method is also found in Quebec and northern Michigan.

Another use of local materials—in this case immediate use. Snowdonia, in North Wales, abounds in stone, slate, and nonconformism. Most Welsh farmers who settled in America came from this area, and most of them could not speak English. Here is The Ugly House in Ty Hyll. It is said to have been built in a day and a night in order for the owner to establish freehold rights to the house and its land. Now mature and charming, the owners don't want to disappoint visitors by tidying up its structure.

Historic precedent says the bigger the roof, the older the building. The saltbox house typifies the shape of historic New England, though the form originated in medieval times. The steeply pitched roof, designed to shed water, resembled the lid of an old-fashioned saltbox when the

rear roof was extended. The addition below the extension was sometimes built of stone. A pleasing feature of some saltbox houses is the slight inward curve of the upper roof as the two sets of timbers meet. The other distinctive shape of this style is the enormous chimney that coped with the fireplaces in each room. Nearer the coast, shingles often covered the walls most exposed to sun and rain. This house in Suffolk County, New York, is—apart from the shingles—almost exactly like the one I was evacuated to in Suffolk, England. Its interior was extremely dark and, like American saltboxes, had small windows. On rainy washdays, clotheshorses in the attic took advantage of the heat that rose through an open trap door to dry the laundry.

Of all the simple house styles, this one defies additional decoration, but—I'm sad to say—not imitation. New saltboxes are dotted here and there in developments, *sans* chimney, completely missing the point of how the building evolved. "Architects" have even designed skylights into the saltbox lids.

Center chimneys needed a lot of thought in their design. The fireplaces they served faced in different directions —sometimes diagonal to each other. Looking at this 1750 Rhode Island chimney, we can see the skilled masonry of the structure-within-a-structure.

Thrifty New Englanders did not waste chimney smoke. Apart from the soot collected to make paint and fertilizer, smoke was used to cure meat. An opening could be made in the chimney as it passed through the attic, and sides of bacon, hams, and sausages would be hung there to be dried and preserved by the smoke.

Space was tight behind the front door of a New England center-chimney home.

The practical and economy-minded Shakers in Maine cover their buildings with what serves best: the side with the worst weather is shingled and creates a bold contrast to the painted clapboards. See how neatly the 1824 Sabbathday Lake Herb House rests on its shaped-stone foundation.

There are many unanswered questions about how the shape of some houses in rural America came to be, especially where people from different countries mingled.

As far as I know, building with logs was not part of the Scotch-Irish history. But as they moved south and then through the Appalachians, they learned the skill from other Protestant folk, such as the Scandinavians and Germans, who were already in Pennsylvania. As they moved west and south, they took the log-building method with them. This is a Tennessee dogtrot house. The dogtrot is the open space between the two evenly sized structures, or cribs, under a common roof. I was impressed with how well this building worked. It allowed for cool breezes in the summer, and the separation of both floors allowed for some privacy. The upstairs

The center of a dogtrot barn in the farmyard.

A look through to the kitchen section of the dogtrot shows its advantages—at least in summer.

landing between the two floors served as a sleeping area on hot nights. Nearly all the family chores could be done in open space, yet under cover. The main room on the left, where the parents also slept, connects to an added kitchen structure behind it. On the right is the parlor, and above are separate rooms for boys and girls. Looking out from the open landing, I could see that the other farm structures were built in the same way, with open space between cribs.

Possible origins. A preserved, 18th-century dogtrot structure in Oslo. I have seen many historic structures like this in Norway, Sweden, and Denmark, often with sod-covered roofs. Settlers in North America remembered this method and used it in the almost treeless High Plains. The edges of the roof are protected by rot-resistant birch bark.

I have never been able to reconcile George Washington's reputation for honesty and the facade of Mount Vernon. The Palladian improvements and enlargements to his farmhouse were finished off with rusticated wooden boards, scored and patterned to make the house appear as though it was built of marble. The style, borrowed from classic Roman architecture, was the latest thing in England before the Revolution. It became very popular on the East Coast of America, but with a difference: the exterior doorways, columns, and arches were frequently made of wood.

Country Interiors

The stark beauty of many American historic rural buildings remains, in my opinion, because there was no original "architect" involved. It is truly folk architecture. There are few plans or drawings. In fact, this prompted the Roosevelt administration to pioneer the Historic American Building Survey in the 1930s. Unemployed trainee architects and students measured and drew threatened farmhouses, barns, mills, churches—all sorts of structures—inside and out. What they learned by doing these fine drawings was how the buildings worked, how they grew, what changes were made, and, in the case of farmhouses and their dependencies, which parts were used and why.

After studying those drawings, I've gained a deeper understanding of the many places I've visited. Over the last ten or so years, I've clambered over many structures, that illustrate in their details the wisdom of the rural men and women. Yes, these places are mostly restored historic farms, and their clocks have stopped. But I encourage you to think of the interiors as genre paintings without the people; imagine these homes with inhabitants, sometimes full of talk and laughter, sometimes miserable, and nearly always working hard at something.

Although I've spent some time trying to save old farm buildings, it's useless to resurrect these vanished scenes as blueprints for living wisely in the country today. Things have changed too much. But there is much here that we can borrow from the past, not only through my factual descriptions, but also by seeing what the light and colors were like; how unpainted and worn objects have a quality that cannot be faked, their form and function being one; that prized possessions, if only just one or two, are placed with care, out of danger, but in full view.

In the American Southwest, the Spanish built with adobe, a method originally brought to them by the invading Moors from North Africa. The very earth where the house stood supplied the mud bricks, mixed with finely shredded straw and dried in the sun. They were laid, from the ground up, like any bricks, with the same muddy mixture used both as mortar and coating for the finished wall. Coating was done by Native American and Hispanic women, originators of the soft-sculpted angles and smooth finishes on the best historic structures in New Mexico.

An adobe building is easy to live with, if you provide minimum care. Attending to its flat roof and the occasional crack on the surface is easy, and the material is at your feet. My friends with adobe houses enjoy doing this because they feel connected to the earth.

The first Hispanic settlers to move up the Rio Grande did not merge with the native population. They were both missionaries and overlords, and the look of their farms, or haciendas, reflects a defensive style. There were thick outside walls for protection against the attacks of unwilling converts, as well as the unrelenting sun. Inside, everything faced a cloistered courtyard, which gave light to the rooms surrounding the quadrangle. The entire structure, called a *ribat*, originated in the Muslim world. This view of the courtyard of the Martinez Hacienda near Taos, shows the well safely inside, and a ladder to provide access to the roof above the entrance.

As is customary when working with adobe, the shapes in this kitchen evolved as trial and error gradually worked out the best size and positions for both cooking hearth and fireplace. Just like kitchens in the East, the first ones in the Southwest had earthen floors, but in the drier climate they were easier to maintain. After being pounded flat, floors were made smooth by continuous wear. Sometimes ox blood was mixed into the mud to provide a harder finish, but the surface was still porous. Periodically, after absorbing large amounts of bacteria from normal living, the floor would have to be dug up. The dirt was valuable, so nitrous that it could be used for the manufacture of gunpowder.

The mistress of the farm looked to her garden for help in making the bedroom a pleasant place. The herbs tansy or pennyroyal, either fresh or dried, would be sprinked between the sheets and mattresses to keep away bedbugs and fleas. Lavender and peppermint were also used to freshen the room with fragrance.

OLD WISDOM

To prevent nightmares, beds should always face from east to west, never from north to south.

You will have bad dreams all the week if you turn the bed on Friday or Saturday. It is unlucky to turn a feather bed on Sunday. Linens clean best if they are pounded with a round-ended wooden beater.

For a long time, until habits and fashions were changed by technology, the master bedroom remained downstairs. Once there were separate rooms downstairs, going upstairs, to what was known as a chamber, was for the rest of the family, or guests. After all, it was cold up there. Those upstairs might have had the benefit of a copper warming pan, which, depending on the part of the country, might be given a comic or bawdy name. This picture shows a change of both heart and times: competing with the bed for pride of place is the chest-on-chest, a valuable possession. The clean, woman's shift and man's shirt are ready for the morning. There was little closet space in the 18th-century house.

What we now call the bed would have been known as a bedstead. The bed itself was a tick, or cloth case, stuffed with feathers, which lay upon a mattress filled with coarser material, such as straw, hay, or hair. This, in turn, rested on ropes strung across the bedstead frame. As I was reminded as a child, you were kept warm in bed by what was underneath; what you piled on top made little difference.

The beautifully worked coverlet is pieced callimanco, or glazed wool. During the day, it is likely that it would have been folded back for cleanliness and to prevent the colors from fading. If this couple had been more prosperous they would have used a bed round, a carpet that went around three sides of the bed and saved the paint work on the floor.

Progress was measured differently in northern Virginia. Away from the rich tidewater lands of the south and east the going was tougher, as this interior reflects. The young homesteader, not being able to afford slaves, would have constructed this dwelling by his own labor. It was built with manageable, untrimmed young logs and local stone. The large gaps between logs were fitted with a mixture of earth and straw. It is just one room, with a sleeping loft reached by a ladder. You can see bedding peeking through the split logs, and every other possession is in view.

Not all farms were seen as a sole occupation. The Oliver Kelley Farm, on the banks of the Mississippi in Elk River, Minnesota, is famous for what its owner did as an absentee. After enduring pioneering first years and a winter with little more than wild rice to eat, Kelley eventually became a government clerk in Washington, D.C., for the Department of Agriculture, and then for the U.S. Postal Service. Keeping the farm back home, he began to organize fellow farmers into a countywide society to pool their knowledge and experiences to become more prosperous and secure. There was little interest in Washington, but his ideas took hold in Minnesota, where the organization became popularly known as the Grange. Farmers could cooperate in the buying of equipment and the selling of the harvest. Today, the nationwide organization continues to advocate on farmers' behalf.

Meanwhile, the Kelley farm was run by his wife, with her two daughters. Like many other women, she played an active role in making a go of it. Note the wooden stair leading down from what was the kitchen, or back, door, to the lean-to, or storage space. If there was more work than the family could handle, this area was the best accommodation they could offer to a hired laborer, who, soon after gathering the fall crops, would pack the trunk near the end of the bed and leave for somewhere warmer. The lean-to had a dirt floor and no insulation. The stove would not be enough to cope with the Minnesota cold.

The root cellar under the house might have been less drafty than the laborer's quarters. It was a modern convenience, directly accessible from the kitchen by inside stairs, unlike the earlier root cellars of New England. The bins could store enough potatoes, beets, and carrots to last well into the following year. They would be placed with care in these bins, between layers of earth to protect them from bruising, rotting and to maintain a constant cool temperature. In the 19th century, pumpkins were mostly grown as cattle feed. These were piled inside to avoid frost damage.

So far we have not seen any carpets or polished and waxed floors. In 1840 in Virginia, farming people would be very happy to walk on fine boards such as these. Considering their heavy use, they were well looked after, frequently swept, and occasionally scrubbed. At least once a year the walls and ceilings would be whitewashed, helping to brighten and sanitize the rooms. There was a difference between the whitewash used inside and out. For inside use, the powdered lime would be mixed with size to prevent it from flaking. But size melts when it gets wet, so it would be useless in the rain. For outside use oil was added to the mixture, which made it waterproof.

The bright, checkerboard-like covering on the floor is what we used to call an oilcloth. A piece of canvas was covered with coats of paint and placed in the area where there was the most traffic. In this case, it is in the middle of the room, where the table would be placed when the family settled down to eat.

Back in the north of Ireland, as late as the turn of the century, things changed slowly. Although there was a window with glass and enough crockery for a large family, life was hard. This was open-plan living, with the best bed tucked under the outshot on the right. A linen cloth above the bed protected it from falling dirt. The use of this bed depended on the circumstance, as the farmer and his wife would give it up for an elderly parent or a sick child. The rest of the family would make do on pallets in front of the hearth, on the settle bed, or in the only other room, which was unheated. All the attention in this one-story building was on the fireplace, built with the best stone and the most care. This was where life was focused. In France, family problems were discussed around the dinner table, sometimes in America, too. In England, such discussions took place at the breakfast table. But in Ireland, at night, the place for talk was the fireside. Those "creepie" stools in the semicircle remained in place most of the time. My Irish relatives used a big trestle table for meals and work, then put it away. Staring into the embers, thoughts were collected and conversation made easy without confrontation.

We have a neighboring farmhouse down the hill. It's a crop and dairy farm that keeps going by using every bit of decent land available and by renting good fields and bottom land within a three-mile radius to supply food for the livestock. The farmhouse is white. It has a porch like this one, and the only time we've seen Leo, the farmer, sitting on it was once when it was pouring rain. Though farmers like rain more than most people, he looked as if he wanted it to stop so he could get moving.

We can see how well-positioned everything is, but also the wear and tear. Although both porch roof and floor generally slope downwards to shed water, there was some dampness affecting the bottom of the posts here. The neat solution was to saw off the offending base and use brackets for support. Past the boot scraper are iron lamp holders to lead people along the boardwalk to the gate in the picket fence. Incidentally, *picket* comes from the French *piquer*, to pierce.

We are led from the garden gate, up the rose-covered, herb-edged path, and over the threshold, which is today just part of the door frame. In the past, a threshold would have been more noticeably higher, built so that it would retain the grains of wheat, barley, or rye that were whacked out of their ears by a flail wielded by someone inside. Of course, most thrashing (threshing) was done on the barn floor, but historically, cottagers would do some at home, too—enough for gruel, or to fatten that special goose.

A typical barn threshold looked like this. The boards would be slotted between posts, and more could be added. A breeze would help things, and another opening on the opposite wall was better still. As they flailed away, the draft of wind through the barn would help to separate the wheat from the chaff.

Throughout the farmland of Holland, apart from the sails of wind pumps, there is the singular shape of the barnhouse. It is seen in Denmark and Germany, too. Considering the number of folk who emigrated from these countries, it is surprising that the style never caught on in America. There is some evidence that the Dutch in the Hudson Valley started to build this way and then abandoned the practice. Maybe it was all that extra land. The separate Dutch-style houses and barns that remain have many similarities to the linked barnhouse. In Holland, the inside was divided into several bays. The end bay—never more than one-third of the building—was the house itself. The advantages of such a compact arrangement can be seen here: no early-morning muddy walks to the cowshed and privy, and the farm wife could run everyday affairs with these inside doors open.

The Country Kitchen

Our largest room is variously called the dining room, kitchen, or workroom. Whatever its name of the moment, it's where we spend most of our time. It was an important factor when we first looked at our house. A very open room, it is full of both morning and afternoon light. It has a step down into the kitchen area, barn-like posts and beams, and a large, brick, corner fireplace. When it is filled with people and the smells of cooking, it has a wonderful ambiance. Guests are invited to sit at the long table facing the fire, away from the cooking area, but some are very happy to sit with their backs warmed by the fire, watching the kitchen-area activity.

The traditional American farm kitchen was not subject to changes in style or character—it was what it was. The biggest and most important room on the farm, the kitchen was where everything was done. It may have been connected to a dairy, pantry, scullery, backhouse, or even an outside bake oven or smokehouse. From this center, a woman would command and control the day-to-day activities of the farm. The kitchen door was located so that she could monitor what was taking place in the working buildings, as well as oversee the garden, orchard, farmyard animals and poultry, and the approach of visitors. All this was done while preparing meals for the family and farm workers, making butter, cheese, and soap, pumping water, and many other daily tasks.

There was rarely time or inclination to use the parlor for a rest. Both men and women, after long working days outside and in, would just want dinner and bed. Parlors were used for special occasions, celebrations, formal gatherings, weddings, and funerals. When portable harmoniums, radios, and televisions first became available, they were considered worthy of special attention in this room.

Today, though the television still occupies an honored place there, most country people live their daily lives with radios and television sets in the kitchen.

How we envision past country life, and think about what it can teach us, has been colored largely by one man and his business activities. In the years before World War I, Wallace Nutting was a successful commercial photographer—a sort of pictorialist—who arranged and sold many photographic scenes (suitable for framing) of how he visualized colonial life and its interiors.With posed models in period dress and authentic settings crammed with genuine antiques and artifacts, these pretty pictures are full of information—and misinformation. His philosophy was, the more the merrier. The more items he included in the scene, the more valuable the items became. (And he owned most of them.) When the silver he used to make prints was commandeered during the war, he was out of business. Nutting then began to manufacture and sell "period" furniture, instigating yet another colonial revival. The furniture was quite well made, but then he overdid things, even designing and marketing "colonial" office equipment.

As time went by, Nutting's work collected some credibility. As more historic places were opened to the public, his photographs were used as reference by a few curators, and many enthusiasts. His legacy is with us today in the attractive, colorful jumble of furniture and artifacts crammed into country kitchens, as seen frequently in decorating magazines. But the way to the truth is through original historic inventories or probate studies, when estates changed hands. There you'll find that most country people had few possessions, and those that they did have were hung for use, not display.

Fifty years ago, the following advice was given:
From
How to Furnish Old American Houses
by Henry L. Williams and Ottalie K. Williams

The Welsh dresser... can have various numbers and arrangements of cupboards and drawers, and the shelves can be used for the better dishes, arranged to display their color and beauty.

Sink-side counters also provide storage space for pots and pans, and a dough trough drawer might provide a place to keep rarely used equipment while the top serves as a stand for a toaster, waffle iron, teapot, coffee pot, or just growing plants under a window.

Spice chests on a wall are useful for holding modern tins of spices, nutmegs, or any of the numerous small objects used in the kitchen. The top might form a shelf for the kitchen clock which of course should be of an early type, perhaps a shelf clock, and certainly not one in the form of a white-painted teapot trimmed with red roses! As in the early living room, wall boxes of various kinds can be used for decorative purposes, particularly spoon racks, knife and candle boxes. Painted tin trays also combine decorative value with utility.

In almost any of these early rooms you can use one or more pieces of French Provincial furniture, providing it is of the simpler character. The natural wood chairs with rush seats have much the same feeling as the early Colonial ladder backs.

In 1726, Susanna Wright, an English Quaker woman, bought one hundred acres on the east bank of the Susquehanna River in Pennsylvania, where she began to farm. Eventually, the family acquired land on the opposite riverbank, which is how Wright's Ferry Mansion got its name. The simple yet elegant stone farmhouse is typical of Quaker households—floors, walls, and windows bare and immaculately maintained throughout. This picture of the kitchen at work invites one to wonder how everything could operate and still remain sparkling clean. The plain mantel fixed to the fireplace's massive bressummer beam by small brackets is not decorative but practical, used as a shelf for pewter dishes and other objects. The beautifully engineered and engraved brass winch secured to the beam turns the iron spit hidden by the table.

The brassware would have been cleaned by rubbing with salt and vinegar; the pewter would have had its sheen restored with a coat of oil, polished with "whitening" on a soft cloth. Both the brick floor and the wooden tabletop are sealed and protected from water, dirt, and scratches by coats of beeswax, buffed by hand. The baskets were probably scrubbed with lye, followed by a rinse of strong salt water.

Children have been at work in this kitchen, sitting at the table for some pre-Halloween carving. The Scotch-Irish had moved westward to the banks of the Tennessee and Cumberland rivers by 1850, and celebrating this time of year had always been part of their history. Pumpkins were unknown in Ireland where, originally, raw turnips were carved. However, it did not take long for the bigger, softer pumpkin to take over.

In summer, the woven splint seat would be thoroughly soaked in water and the chair would then be hung upside down in the sun to dry. This would make the sagging disappear. The kitchen is an extension of a log house and built in the same rough-and-ready way. The ladder leads to a loft, where winter foodstuff is stored.

As she adjusted to life on the frontier, the farmer's wife tried to make the best of things. Although little could be done to alter appearances, modern conveniences arrived, including the new sash window and its curtains, store-bought pickle barrels, and a fine new pie safe with screened doors, and drawers underneath.

The cookstove, sensibly raised on squared-off timbers, kept the dust from wood ash to a minimum. It would also heat water for the children's hip bath, which would be placed in front of it on cold winter nights.

There have been more inventions to ease kitchen labor than any other area of the home. The three-legged chopping block is one that has remained unchanged for hundreds of years. Made of hardwood and easy to scrub, many have outlasted generations of families.

By 1900, the design of farmhouses and their satellite buildings was affected by the women who were responsible for not only family and domestic matters but also the efficiency of the whole complex. Mail-order manufacturers of buildings, machinery, and hardware paid special attention to their needs and criticisms. In this progressive era, periodicals such as *The American Agriculturist* and *The American Farmer* printed plans contributed by women. These journals published their shared experiences of life on farms all over the country, full of household tips to increase efficiency. The woman operating the kitchen of this Iowa farm divided her work area into thirds: a main kitchen, a back kitchen, and a long connecting pantry. This partitioning allowed for extra shelving and more work surfaces. The fully operational stove is still in use today and demonstrates considerable output and versatility. A labor-saving potato ricer sits on the easy-to-wipe tablecloth. In warm weather, everyone would have appreciated the new screen door, considering the heat generated by the black and silver "Acorn Utility."

For around $20 ($4 extra for a porcelain top) and about $3 for freight, the back kitchen would get a Hoosier cabinet, described as follows:

A Cabinet Makes Your Day's Work Lighter and Shorter.

It is arranged to bring everything you need within a space smaller than your kitchen table.

Sturdily built of well-seasoned oak; sliding top of white porcelain or nickeled metal.

You will have plenty of room for dishes, bowls, and jars in the china closet.

Large sized flour bin on left side has metal sifter.

Sliding top can be pulled out—gives you a space 40" long and 35" wide to do your work on.

Under the sliding top is a cutting board which pulls out with top.

Block for attaching meat chopper on right side of sliding top.

In the bottom are two drawers where you can keep cutlery and many other small things you need in your work in the kitchen.

The large drawer at bottom has metal bread and cake box with sliding metal lid.

Base cupboard has sliding metal shelf and pan rack.

Three-ply bottom base with substantially built framework.

Height 68" Width 40"
Depth 25".
Shipping Weight 220 lbs.

By 1865, German-speaking peoples began to arrive in large numbers. Settling for the most part in the northern and central states, they tended to stick together in their own regional groups. They traveled light, having to sell everything to make the journey.

This is the kitchen of Mathais Schottler's lonely looking farm on page 76. By 1875, the log walls had been plastered over, and it contained a number of new utensils that fit the six plates of the Royal Atlantic stove. Placing the stove in the center of the room, as the Shakers would, made it easier to use and allowed the heat to radiate better. The scuttle of coal under the bench supplied more heat than wood. On a cold washday, the larger linens and clothes would dry upstairs in the attic.

The "best" china displayed on the worn dresser shelves reminds me of an old photograph. A new farmer, his wife, and children are standing outside a sod-and-log house out on the prairie. Beside them is a rocking chair, a grandmother clock, and a bird in a cage. Resting on the seat of the chair is a china vase. The children hold the bridles of a horse and two cows. They all are wearing their Sunday best, their expressions stiff as they wait for the exposure. They look as if they are being evicted. In fact, they were posed by an itinerant photographer so they could send proud evidence to family back home of how well things were going.

The kitchen of Hildene, the Vermont home of Robert Todd Lincoln, shows some of the gadgets invented in the late 19th and early 20th centuries. In the background is a knife cleaner. Stiff bristles inside the drum removed grime and rust from the steel blades as the drum turned. Enameled containers were popular for keeping dried foodstuffs, and their hard coating made washing colanders, pots, and saucepans easier. Electricity had been installed, and the dependable iron stove acquired a smoother profile, when it no longer needed to generate heat for the kitchen. It has a warming compartment with sliding covers and purpose-built tools to operate the plates and doors. With its brass hanging rail, it looks like a forerunner of the much-loved (and expensive) Aga cookers of present-day English country homes.

A modern Aga stove, very much at home among 300-year-old beams.

The Finns ended up working harder at settling Wisconsin than did other Nordic peoples. Most of them were late arrivals in the immigrant boom at the turn of the last century. The only land left for these desperately poor folk was worn-out "cutovers," remaining from a logging boom in the far north of the state. In Finland there had been widespread unemployment, even starvation, for a population firmly under the thumb of czarist Russia. When compulsory military service was imposed on the men, something had to be done. Rather than comply, many left, hoping to pay back the cost of the steamship ticket by succeeding in the New World.

Would-be farmers left a country where only ten percent of the land was tillable and no farm was larger than twenty acres. They did not set their sights high, disciplined in the Old Country to perform even the most dismal jobs. What they brought with them was an incredible spirit of purpose. They had no money to buy land; to get that money, they became miners, stonecutters, and lumberjacks.

The "cutover" land bought by the Finns was covered with stumps, brush, and stones. Beneath was poor soil and barely enough humus to sustain their first crops; but they made a go of it. After building the good new life, a farming family would be able to have a sauna and other things important in Finnish culture, things they only dreamed of before. Their farmhouses grew easily, because they preferred a modular system, adding complete log sections to existing structures.

This is the inside of the Ketola family farmhouse, first raised in Bayfield County around 1894. It shows the advantage of unfinished log walls, which can take any number of nails, hooks, and wooden pegs without changing character. In the harsh Wisconsin winters, Finns moved easily on home-carved skis. If you look closely at the homemade boots beside the dry sink, you'll notice that the pointed toes turn up to fit securely in ski bindings, yet allow the boots to slip free in an accidental fall.

The stove is an example of Victorian over-decoration. The manufacturers, claiming a combination of aesthetics and efficiency, maintained that "the more surfaces there are, the more heat is broadcast."

Below stairs in Louisiana, an enthusiastic cook renovated this magnificent kitchen of an antebellum plantation house, upriver from New Orleans. Local cypress was employed to make the square table, which is really a work station because of its height and position. We can see the cooking areas of three different periods. The original hearth in the center is now barely filled by the Franklin stove, with a top that serves as a hot plate. On the right is an iron stove for slow cooking and baking, and on the left is a modern countertop with electric burners. The owner had been impressed by the use of niches in the Southwest, and these provide a source of light to the far corners of the kitchen.

The wisdom of country furniture lies in its strength, the use of its materials, and its versatility after years of continuing use. Chests, chairs, tables, beds, and some clever combinations of them all have their stories.

Drawers in old chests were dovetailed in all four corners to slide and stay flush despite changes in humidity. Before a piece left the workshop, the furniture maker would rub a bar of soap along the sides and edges of the drawers so that they would slide even more smoothly.

Country Furniture

I know that the first child born in Plimoth Colony was rocked to sleep aboard the anchored *Mayflower* in a wicker cradle while his father worked to build the first shelters. But probably the earliest piece of furniture to land was a simple lidded chest containing precious worldly goods. It is likely to have been painted in two colors with carving on the front and sides, and with initials—most certainly a wife's, and perhaps her husband's as well—engraved in the front. This box had a symbolic and legal meaning: it was a dower chest, evidence of a wife's rights in the marriage contract. It qualifies as furniture rather than luggage because the corner posts had been slightly extended to become legs.

Over the years, a bottom drawer or two was added to the dower chest. Hence the habit of the bride-to-be to put things away in those drawers for her future marriage. Eventually the chest became all drawers, and waited for another to be stacked on top. (My mother, who came from a busy family of eleven children, reminded me that her first crib as an infant was a bottom drawer placed on two facing chair seats.) The same early chest sometimes opened in the front, and later, with shelves above, became a hutch, or dresser. After living with stools and benches, country people were glad to rest their backs and arms on chairs. They weren't fancy, but their shape indicated that someone local had the use of a lathe to turn the legs and supporting stretchers. The trestle, or sawbuck, table was basically a board supported by a standard, or x- shaped trestle. Styles were those the makers remembered from England, but they were constructed with the plentiful native woods.

Using a variety of woods to fit the purpose, and not caring about matching grain and color, has always suited country people. The wood for the bent back of a chair might be different from the wood for the seat, and the legs might come from a young trunk of still another wood of greater strength—the chair would be painted anyway. When there was the surprise of a new wood, it was used to best advantage. For example, the uniquely American tiger maple revealed its wonderful horizontal patterns only after it was sawn for lumber; it was hard to resist making whole pieces of furniture from it.

My favorite pieces of furniture are combinations that conserved limited space and gave protection from cold drafts. The hutch table could be a table and a chest and sometimes a settle. The tabletop, round or square, was held in place by dowels and could be raised to form a solid chair back; the lid of the chest became the seat.

The best country furniture was made by carpenters rather than by cabinetmakers. Over time, woodworking terms from the Old World and the New have changed their meanings slightly. An English joiner was, in America, a carpenter. In England, a cabinetmaker made fancy cabinets. In America, a good carpenter could work on the massive proportions of timber-framed buildings and also—like Shaker brothers—design built-in cupboards and fashion the dovetails of a clock case.

Almost none of the original furniture made for the first cottage rooms is available now, and what still exists is very expensive. Easier to find—and afford—are the old mail-order chairs, tables, and cabinets that replaced the painted items. We have a cherry and maple table with ten matching chairs that my wife's great-grandparents had when they set up a home on the family farm in the late 1870s. It seats from four to twelve comfortably, as it expands in increments of a foot when leaves are added — another form of family planning. Occasionally, we polish the table with a paste wax to protect it from water and other spills. Sometimes, when one of the chair seats needs reweaving, I think we should replace them all, but since I've seen them in antiques shops, I know that replacements are not far away.

There must have been thousands shipped out by Sears, Roebuck & Co. Later farm furniture, sturdily constructed, became chunky, and much of it has a very prominent chestnut or oak grain that I don't like, but flea marketeers love.

Today there are more and more woodworkers throughout the United States making fine country furniture following original patterns. Some furniture kits available, particularly of Shaker pieces, are of very good value.

There has been a halt in the decline in the numbers of Shaker brothers and sisters in the last few years with additions to the community at Sabbathday Lake in Maine. Neither does the spirit of Shaker design fade in or near other Shaker villages as expert woodworkers continue the tradition of making this elegant, simple, and useful furniture. Another group, the Amish, is growing steadily. If you are lucky enough to be within travelling distance of their homes, Amish journeymen carpenters will rebuild or restore your ailing structures. Fine Amish-made furniture is available throughout the East and Midwest. Their designs are refinements of country pieces. Furniture designers, such as Thomas Moser, have distilled these classic American art forms even further into beautiful, spare furniture for contemporary use. In all, awareness of the history of country people and the materials they used is on the increase. Although a Shaker sister said that she did not want to be remembered as a chair, she did know, as Thomas Merton said, that it was made by someone capable of believing that an angel would like to sit in it.

One of Thomas Jefferson's many inventions, this silver candleholder enabled him to continue reading in a favorite chair once natural light had diminished.

This stout old hutch dresser shows signs of continual wear. It tells the story of a German family kitchen so busy that the door's worn fastenings are replaced as work goes on. I have seen reproduction painted furniture with stress marks here and there, but I doubt if the finishers could bring something off as convincing as this.

Historic Deerfield, in Massachusetts, is a fine place to see how village life went on in the 1700s. The curators have avoided the temptation to clutter the interiors. Instead, they have looked at the probate records of property ownership and inventories. This was what the kitchen furnishings looked like on a day in 1725. Leaning on the outside bricks is a peel, used to place and retrieve loaves of bread from the oven in the back. Also shown are a lug pole with three hooks on which to hang the iron pot, a pair of tongs, and a brass kettle, along with a two-pronged fork hanging from the bressummer beam, another knife and fork, two skillets with legs, an adze, an axe, and two sacks of grain.

This upstairs pantry was, by rural standards, very well equipped, with typical wooden plates and bowls stored with an eye for convenience.

Two sets of initials are on display in this Massachusetts chamber. The maker of the big chest probably also painted it—the decorations are inspired doodles showing the use of his own compass and rule. The simple initials of Mistress Katson King balance his efforts on the upper drawer. Resting on the chest, in a place of honor, is a Bible box.

The walls are interesting because they show how things looked before fashions changed. By the 19th century, walls like this would have been plastered and covered with wallpaper. Anyone lucky enough to have them today would most likely leave them like this. The problem with such large boards is that they would be completely spoiled by 20th-century sockets, holes, and wiring. But as they are not load bearing and simply cover the studs, it's easy to move them somewhere else so that they remain untouched. They can be replaced with less precious material.

The multipurpose, scrubbed-pine dresser on a wall opposite the hearth would be the other main focus in the kitchen. With the family crockery on display, it could also be thought of as the picture-and-sculpture gallery. In the north of Ireland, dressers like this would be the home of the local Belleek mugs shown here; each in its proper space, washed and replaced by its owner. The design of the unit evolved as shelf heights were positioned to accommodate various objects.

Below, one drawer would be for knives, forks, and spoons, the other for overflow and a pair of scissors, pencil, papers, and string long enough to be saved. The bottom compartments had many uses in English, Irish, and Welsh dressers. They might even become the home to newly born puppies, kittens, and chicks, and, sometimes the kennel for a retired sheepdog.

When an old cottage is restored and the studs and braces are exposed, some owners cannot resist the temptation to fill in the gaps. Note the horse brasses alternating with china bric-a-brac on the central posts.

The difference between having things on a dresser for display and putting them away neatly after use is illustrated by this smart, glass-fronted kitchen cupboard. The cups hang on hooks in front of plates that can be easily reached.

Beds

Staying as a guest in a country room with a four-poster bed is an attraction for city people and worth a detour for weekenders. Four-posters, however, were not typical in most historic farmhouses. Before the 1800s, nearly everyone slept on a simple frame, strung with rope to support a mattress. After the 1730s, mostly in towns and among well-off landowners, ceilings rose above eight feet in height, and made four-posters popular until about 1835. The four posts were connected at the top by a frame, or tester, from which hung a valance, often matching the pattern of the curtains below. The curtains were an extra measure of draft protection and privacy, making the bed a chamber in itself. I recall a Shaker room where an outside wall next to the bed was covered with a large sheet of linen, hanging neatly from the pegboard, as protection against the winter cold.

Eventually, the ropes were replaced by boards, making it easier to slide a space-saving trundle bed underneath. The Victorians, in their passion to use industrial solutions to solve domestic problems, argued that wood was unhygienic, full of disease-carrying bugs—and gave us the brass bedstead. For a quarter of the price, you could have iron, with brass knobs. Bed curtains in the form of netting were used before the invention of window screens. These were understandably popular on the four-poster, and even the half-tester, in the South. Though Gloucestershire in England is not known for hot, insect-filled nights, a homemade half-tester here is squeezed under the eaves of a cottage, enabling the skylight windows to remain open in the summer.

A neat "turn-up" bedstead rests against a kitchen wall in Massachusetts. Leaning against the head of the bed is a wrench to tighten the frequently sagging ropes. After being inserted through the gap between the rope and the frame's outside, it twisted, and thus tightened, the rope.

As they moved west, pioneers had to make their own rough bedsteads. In the corner of a dirt-floor cabin, a bed-width away from the walls, a stout, forked stick would be driven firmly into the ground. Two poles resting at right angles would be forced into the log walls to give support to rails that would support the sleepers on their bedding filled with hay or moss. It is not surprising that there is little evidence of these beds today.

A cozily curtained four-poster fits into a chamber bedroom. Underneath the 18th-century linsey-woolsey coverlet is a bolster, commonly used with separate pillows, to prop up the sleeper and lessen pulmonary complaints.

Less massive, and with a more open, airy feeling, was the field, or tent, bedstead of the early 1800s, with its arched frame for the canopy. This design was influenced by the sleeping arrangements of officers in the field, although twin beds were rare before 1900.

A mushroom slat-back chair

An early German side chair with leather seat

An early Pennsylvania bannister-back armchair

A bow-back Windsor armchair

A Shaker side chair

Country Chairs

Just like their houses, the earliest furniture for country people was overbuilt—particularly chairs. Massive, solid-backed, throne-like armchairs gradually gave way to bannister- and ladder-back designs that culminated in the very best Windsor and Shaker chairs. Their builders knew that the weakest part of a chair was where the seat and back joined. The Windsors showed a number of variations of the delicately tapering spokes that support a sitter's back. These spokes rose to meet tops that had shapes generally described as bow, loop, comb, fan, and hoop back. Sometimes braces were employed to give further support, producing a fine example of thrust and counterthrust.

The Shakers made their chairs with combined posts and legs. They solved the stress problem by having this seemingly upright design lean back slightly so that weight would be transferred to the base of the rear legs, where wooden ball-and-socket "tilter" feet took the strain as the sitter leaned back. These tilters were held in place by a thin leather thong attached to the inside of the leg. The Shakers invented this design because they found it hard to tolerate the dents that cherry or maple legs would make on their bare, shining, pine floorboards.

Wallace Nutting, knowledgeable about colonial furniture, in his book *American Windsors*, describes a Windsor as "a stock-leg chair, with a spindle back topped by a bent bow or comb. On a good Windsor, lightness, strength, grace, durability and quaintness are all found in an irresistible blend." He goes on to say, "Construction of the Windsor involves many delicate adjustments and could only be made in fine form by specially trained men. For instance, the seat slants backward. The arm rail slants still more. The bow, when bored for the spindles, is very much cut away and will break unless the best wood, carefully worked, is used." A good chair would be made in tension. The maker knew that extreme stress would be imposed on the components when they were joined. A leg or spindle wedge driven too loosely would not tighten the tenon; one driven too hard would split the leg, arm, or seat. From tension came strength.

Even though many factories produced the same type of chair, Lambert Hitchcock (1795-1852) became associated with painted chairs with a stencilled design because, early on, he made a practice of labeling his chairs. He made a variety of chairs, such as slat-backs, arrow-backs, Boston rockers, and simple armchairs. The generic "Hitchcock" sometimes includes early Sheraton chairs, which were painted in light colors and had handpainted decorations. By 1820, stencils were used on these chairs, and they were painted in darker colors such as black, brown, green, and pumpkin.

Ladder-back (also called slat-back) chairs originated in England, and were being made in this country by the end of the 1600s. It is a simple design, much liked by country craftsmen, with four or five horizontal slats across a high back. Early chairs, often painted, were made with rush, and later splint, seats; the Shakers used woven tape.

The rocking chair, a classic example of American country furniture, dates from the mid-18th century, when rockers were attached to existing chairs. The curved pieces of wood were attached to the chair by a groove cut into the bottom of the chair leg, or by either pegging or bolting the rocker to the outside of the leg. At first, rockers had the same measurement both in the front and the back, but later the back became longer. From the 1850s on, many rockers were constructed of maple, had a natural finish, and were factory made.

A rare bow-back Windsor armchair from Maryland. It has a comb extension above the crest rail and bamboo-style legs.

A comb-back Windsor armchair

A Windsor armchair with bamboo-style legs

A Boston rocker

A Hitchcock side chair

An 1870s side chair with cane seat

The first Shaker's chair. Mother Ann Lee, founder of the Shakers, used this Windsor chair when she stayed at Harvard, Massachusetts. You can see that rockers have been added to the legs. It was made before the Shakers began making furniture for their own use and for the "World's People." The comb-back, or stick-back, style of chair got its name from the town of Windsor in the county of Berkshire, England, which was famous for furniture making.

A bannister-back side chair from a 17th-century Connecticut house.

In Ireland, there is always a *curaird* chair placed inside the back door of every farmhouse. It's an invitation for a visitor to come in and pull the chair to the fire. A tradition in the West, a *curaird,* or visit, is informal and always welcome. The value of your visit is that you bring news. When it is time to leave, you put the chair back where it was. As a child, I was told that if you pick up a chair once, you do it twice.

This chair back, with its nicely engraved lettering, is a simpler version of other crested, bannister-back chairs made in northeast Massachusetts. The curved top and the commemoration to Priscilla Capen, the parson's wife, is very much in the style of the local gravestones. The connection of the date to events in her life is not known.

A Country Workplace

Here, in what used to be Shaker country, there is still an awareness of their skills and traditions. All Shaker brothers had trades, and some had two, or even three or four. Everyone took his part in the village business, farming, building, gardening, smithy work, skilled carpentry, and furniture making. They believed in a variety of labor, seeing it as a source of pleasure and satisfaction. A friend of mine, who is an enthusiastic blacksmith, carver, and woodworker, had this Shaker-influenced wall bench made by a local craftsman. My friend is also following their example of a proper home for each tool, and their founder's maxim "that there is no dirt in heaven."

Among the many fine tools visible in this picture some have a particular connection to the buildings and furniture of rural America.

On the extreme left, two augers hang in their racks on the bottom peg rail. An auger drilled the holes for pegs that held the beams and posts of barns and houses together.

At the top of the wooden post and brace is a traveller. This was used by wheelwrights to measure the length of a rounded surface so that a new tire could be fitted.

Just below it and to the right of the beam is a slick that made surfaces flush, as when pegs protruded in post-and-beam construction. To the right of the slick in the same rack are chisels used by carpenters to fashion the mortises for doorlocks.

On the rack slightly above and to the right is a 125-year-old hand drill that a careful woodworker would use to make a nail hole slightly thinner than the nail itself. When the nail was driven home in thick pieces of timber, the extra space stopped the wood from splitting.

In the middle of the picture is an 18th century German goosewing axe that found its way to the New World, and a hand-forged French axe, to its right, to make wooden legs.

To the right and slightly above the plover is the versatile Stanley 55 Plane. It came with fifty-five interchangeable blades so that every planing task could be handled.

Hanging from the post under the bow saw is a long joiner plane. This would be used to level surfaces where two floorboards joined.

The big saw slightly below and far right is a powerful metal-handled dock saw that when properly sharpened would make short work of a thick plank.

Caring for Furniture

Old furniture acquires a beautiful patina over time. It is a look acquired after years of exposure to sunlight, air, polishing, and use. The wood becomes colored with a subtlety unmatched by stain from a can. There are still pieces of furniture, to be found in antiques stores or at auctions, whose original patina can be preserved. This is especially true of mahogany, walnut, maple, or cherry with an old finish. It's important to decide if a piece of furniture can be restored, because stripping will remove in minutes what took years to create.

If your piece of furniture looks as if the original finish might be retained, the first step is to clean it thoroughly to get rid of the years of accumulated dirt and grease. Start by dipping a cotton cloth in a solution of equal parts mineral oil, turpentine, and white vinegar to remove dirt and old wax. Squeeze the excess from the cloth, and rub with the grain. Test a small, concealed area in order to see what effect this has on the finish. Then you will know how to proceed with the rest of the surface. Wipe a small section at a time, and dry with a clean cotton cloth before going on to the next section. Give the whole piece another wipe with a fresh cloth, and let it dry for at least twenty-four hours. Next, apply one or two thin coats of good quality paste wax, buffing well after each coat.

Often you will find furniture with old shellac or varnish that is sticky. In this case, use #0000 steel wool, which is very fine. Dip a steel wool pad in mineral spirits and rub lightly along the grain of the wood, removing only the build-up of dirt and wax, not the finish. Follow by wiping with a soft cotton cloth. If there is good coverage left, polish with paste wax, and buff. However, if the old finish disappears, you might want to refinish.

You may find a chest that has been stored in a humid place, and the drawers might smell musty. To remedy this, remove any paper linings, vacuum thoroughly, then air the drawers for several days, preferably in sunlight. Next, place a saucer of baking soda in each drawer, replace the drawers in the chest, and let stand for a week, refreshing the baking soda if necessary. If this does not solve the problem, you can sand the insides of the drawers and paint on a coat of sealer to lock in the smell.

White spots or rings on a table or chest are caused by water and indicate the water did not go all the way through the finish. You might be able to remove the marks by sprinkling table salt on the spot and then rubbing gently—always with the grain—with a cloth dampened with mineral oil. The abrasion will dull the finish a bit, but you can bring back the shine with paste wax.

Cracks in wood surfaces, produced by use and dry conditions, can be filled with wood putty. Powdered putty is the recommended type because it will absorb a stain to match the old wood. Follow the mixing instructions, force it into the cracks, and smooth out. When it is hard and dry, sand and stain.

In rural areas, furniture was usually constructed by farmers and settlers themselves to serve a need and to fit a specific place. For example, corner cupboards were built to fit, then painted not only to protect the wood but also to add color to a plain room. At first, country furniture was painted reddish brown, brown, or black, followed later by blue, green, gray, or ochre. These colors came from berries, organic matter, or clays mixed with water, milk, or linseed oil. For example, reds were created from berries or powdered iron oxide, which could produce shades of red-brown, light red, and maroon; black could be obtained by mixing chimney soot with linseed oil. During the 18th century, painted furniture was embellished with various patterns created by the use of feathers, combs, and sponges. At the same time, these techniques, along with stencils, were used on walls in the house.

If you find a piece of furniture that you think is truly old, remember that it should have a faded look after years of exposure to sun and dirt, and it should also show signs of wear. Look carefully, because wear can be faked with steel wool. Old paint, if scraped, comes as powder, but new paint will come off in pieces or ribbons. Also, check the underside of the piece as well as the back, and be suspicious—especially if there is paint where a frugal country person would not waste it.

Saw marks help tell the story of a piece of furniture, especially its age. Early marks were straight, made by saws driven by windmills and waterwheels. Then, around 1850, the circular saw powered by steam engines came into use. This type of saw left curved marks. Nails and screws also help determine the age of furniture. Hand-forged nails were pointed and had round or rectangular heads. By 1815, machinery came along that made nails with square heads and blunt ends. These were used until the end of the 1800s, when round-headed nails with pointed ends came on the scene. The first screws were made of hand-cut wood; they were replaced by machine-made screws at the beginning of the 1800s. These screws had even threads and blunt ends. Pointed ends came into use in the second half of the 1800s.

This Windsor chair was given to us by a friend. Her husband, who used it every day for more than forty years, gradually wore off the original finish and polished the bare wood on the arms to give them a lovely golden glow.

Many chairs were made with cane, rush, or splint seats, which eventually sag from use. To tighten, soak the underside of the seat with water and hang it upside down. As the natural material dries, it should tighten and make the chair usable again.

In most cases, wood furniture originally was painted for a purpose, often to disguise a mixture of secondary woods or unappealing woods or common pine. This is true for furniture ranging from Windsor chairs of the 1700s to Hoosier kitchen cabinets in the 1800s. For example, some chairs and Hoosier cabinets were made from four or five different kinds of wood, then painted. What makes these painted pieces appealing is not the wood but the finish that often has acquired a lovely patina over the years. They can be cleaned in sections by wiping lightly with an equal solution of turpentine and mineral oil (years ago called paraffin oil), and then drying with clean cloths. The surface can then be sealed by waxing. If a piece is too battered to clean, it is better to repaint than to refinish.

Chair Repair

There is a great deal of stress where the seat of a chair joins the back. If this joint becomes loose, the two pieces move when the chair is used, and other joints start to loosen. A rung is usually first to be affected by the motion and will work its way out of the leg.

The old glue on the end of the rung and inside the fitting can be softened by pouring hot vinegar on it. Any glue that does not dissolve after a few minutes can be gently scraped off, and the area can then be dried.

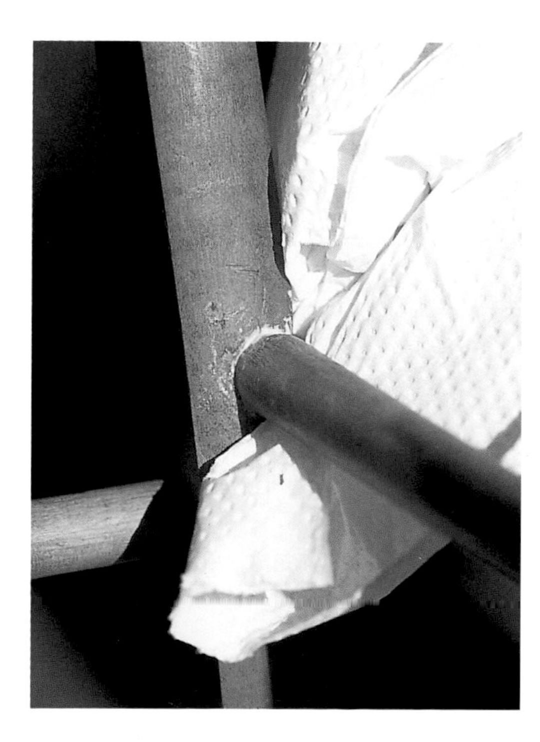

Next, carpenter's wood glue should be applied and the rung placed back in its hole. Carefully remove all excess glue.

Hold the two pieces firmly together while the glue dries; tie with rope or use a bungee cord.
Wait twenty-four hours before using.

This is a view of the lean-to kitchen at the 1660 Thomas Lee House in coastal Connecticut, showing a ship's knee brace supporting the beam. The room is remarkably unchanged. The Shakers, who invented the flat broom, always hung them like this. It does not take long for a broom that stands on the floor to lose its shape, the spring in its bristles, and its effectiveness. In a different environment, the oak floor could be preserved and have the cracks filled in the following way:

Soak some newspaper in water, mash it into pulp, squeeze it out, and put it in a bucket. Then mix powdered glue with water in a separate container until it is smooth and flowing. Add the glue to the pulp, stirring well, and blend into the mixture a dry earth color that matches the filler to the floorboard. Place in the cracks, remove the excess, and let the floor dry thoroughly before sanding.

Country Household Hints

Gathered from books published in the 19th century, such as Mrs. Child's *The American Frugal Housewife*, are selected items of household advice that show how things were kept clean and sparkling. They are presented here, in large part, as they were written. Indeed, many of these natural cleaners are still effective.

Baskets
Appy equal parts of boiled linseed oil and turpentine to baskets to clean and prevent drying. Then wipe off excess with a dry cloth.

To clean, first scrub with lye from the wash tub, and then rinse with strong salt water.

Brass
Crushed coarse rhubarb leaves will clean both brass and copper.

Mix equal parts of salt and flour and moisten with vinegar to make a thick paste. Apply with a damp cloth. Then wash and dry.

Shine unvarnished beds with half a lemon dipped in salt. After washing and drying, rub the brass with rottenstone (Note: this is a finely ground natural limestone powder).

Rottenstone and oil are proper materials for cleaning brasses. If wiped every morning with flannel and New England rum, they will not need to be cleaned half as often.

Brooms
To make a new broom last longer, soak in hot salt water before using.

Carpets
Cut the heart of a cabbage in half. Using it like a brush, go over the carpet to clean.

Coat grease spots with a layer of cornmeal, rub into the carpet and let stand overnight. Then brush up cornmeal.

To sweep carpets clean, first sprinkle with fresh grass clippings or with fresh, dry powder snow.

Clean a dirty carpet by scattering grated raw potatoes and then brushing vigorously.

Copper
To remove tarnish, clean it with half a lemon dipped in a mixture of one tablespon of salt and one tablespoon of vinegar.

Crush a raw onion with damp earth and use as a polish.

Dampen an old cloth and rub fine sand on the pieces until they gleam. Procure very fine sand from ant hills.

Dampness
To reduce dampness in closets, wrap twelve pices of chalk together and hang them up.

Fireplace
When the fire is burning brightly, toss in a handful of salt to act as a cleaner.

To remove soot and grit from inside the chimney, place a couple handfuls of common bay salt hay on the fire.

Floors
Clean varnished floors and woodwork with cold tea to bring out their shine.

Before sweeping a dusty floor, sprinkle with damp tea leaves, or fresh grass cuttings. They will collect the dust, and prevent it from rising onto the bedding and furniture.

Furniture
To remove minor white marks from wooden furniture, rub with a paste made of olive oil mixed with cigar ashes. Then polish off with a soft cloth.

To blend in small surface scratches, rub with the broken edge of a piece of walnut meat and polish with a soft cloth.

Give a fine soft polish to varnished furniture by rubbing with pulverized rottenstone and linseed oil, and afterwards wipe clean with a soft silk rag.

Glass
Clean a glass bottle or decanter by filling with soapy water and adding a couple tablespoons of vinegar.

Wipe crystals from chandelier with two parts vinegar to three parts water, then rinse and dry.

Gold
Polish gold by using a soft cloth and a paste made of cigar ashes and water.

Ice
Put hay on icy steps in the winter to prevent slipping. Keep a bale beside the door you ordinarily use. It won't track into the house like ashes or salt.

Knives
Clean and polish the blades with fireplace ashes.

Leather
Clean leather by rubbing with equal parts of vinegar and boiled linseed oil, and then polish with a cloth.

Beat the whites of three eggs and rub them with a soft cloth into a leather chair. The leather will soon be clean and shine as if new.

Odor
Simmer vinegar on the stove to get rid of unpleasant cooking odors.

Put out a cut onion and leave until it has drawn unpleasant smells to itself and then throw it away.

Paint
Hardened paint on brushes can be softened by soaking in boiling vinegar. Afterwards wash in hot soapy water.

Remove paint from glass by applying hot vinegar with a cloth. After it is softened, scrape off gently.

Pests
To keep ants away from the house, sprinkle dried and powdered leaves of tansy and pennyroyal on doorsteps and window ledges.

Freshly cut pennyroyal placed in a room, or drops of oil sprinkled about, will keep away mosquitoes.

Tansy or pennyroyal will keep away fleas. Rub cats and dogs with fresh-cut pennyroyal once a week.

When bedbugs lodge in the wall, fill any apertures with a mixture of soft soap and snuff. Take the bedstead apart and treat in the same way.

Make flypaper by spreading on paper a mixture of melted resin and enough lard or oil to make it, when cold, the consistency of honey.

A muslin bag filled with pounded cloves and placed on the pantry shelf will keep flour and grains free of weevils.

To keep moths away, procure shavings of cedar wood, enclose in muslin bags, and place in chests, drawers, and closets with woolen clothing.

Pewter
When polish is gone off, first rub on the outside with a little sweet oil (olive oil) on a piece of soft linen; then clear oil off with pure whiting (powdered chalk) on linen cloths.

Silver
Soak tarnished silverware in sour milk for half an hour. Then wash in soapy water and dry.

Soak tarnished silver in potato water for several hours.

For scratches use a paste of olive oil and whiting and rub with a soft cloth.

Make a paste of baking soda and water and scrub with a soft brush.

Stains
Moisten fruit stains with glycerine, let stand for several minutes and rinse.

Hold fabric with stains from berries and juices over a basin and pour boiling water through. Then wash with soap and rinse.

Dip clothing with fresh bloodstains in salted water, to remove or diminish stain.

Tea-stained cloth should be rubbed with a mixture of one tablespoon of salt and one cup of soft soap and then placed outside in the sun for a day, before laundering.

Wallpaper
Make a smooth paste of equal parts of cornstarch and water and rub on wallpaper spots. When it is dry, brush off and spots will be gone.

Wax
Place a blotter on candle wax, and then hold a hot iron over the blotter which will absorb the melted wax.

Windows
To clean, rub down with kerosene on newspapers. Especially good for rain spots.

Wash with a mixture of one part vinegar to ten parts warm water.

The always busy, clean, and efficient kitchen at Hancock Shaker Village.

Country Remedies

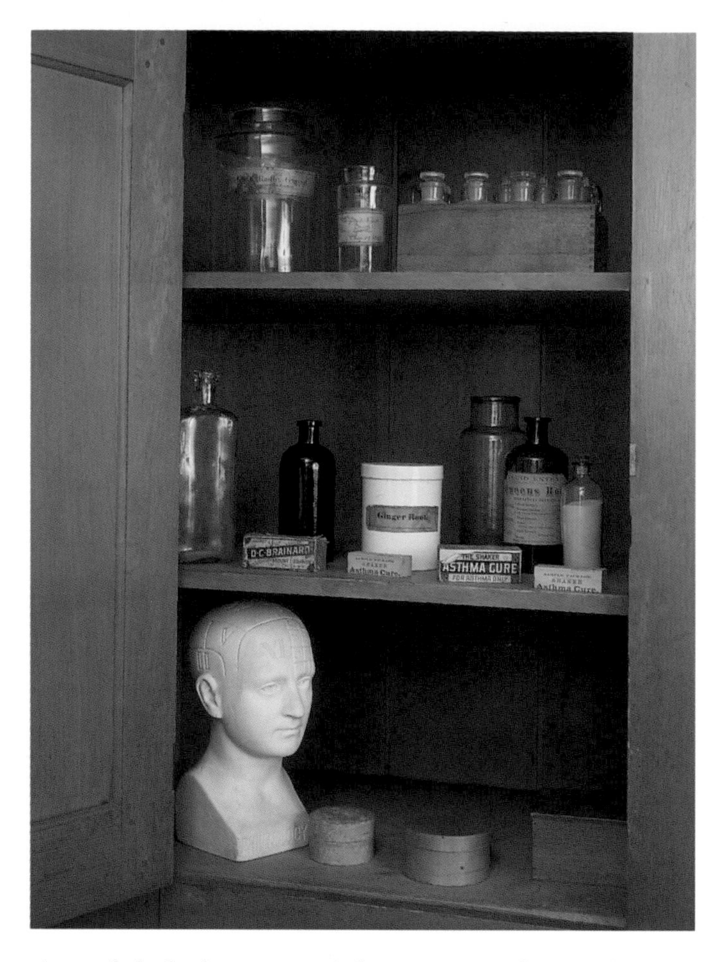

A good deal of country wisdom concerns how to look after various aches, pains, and ailments. Since doctors were few and far between, families had to care for themselves.They looked to the advice that was handed down through the generations from their own immigrant group, and from the Native Americans in their area. Included here—mostly as written—are some examples of American folk medicine and folklore commonly found in old sources. Some are delightful and probably worked due to the placebo effect, while others—those using herbs or fruits—may actually have beneficial effects. Then there are some remedies that simply sound outrageous. You might recall hearing one or two of the following cures mentioned in your own family. I should also add that these remedies are to be relished for their interest, rather than heeded.

Abscess or Boil
Tie bread in a white cloth, dip it in boiling water and place on the abscess overnight.

Press a cabbage leaf dipped in hot water on the abscess.

Cover the area with a slice of onion, and wrap with a clean cloth.

Apply a poultice made of crushed burdock leaves, or one made of ginger and flour, to draw boil to a head.

Bruises
Treat a bruise by applying brown paper coated with molasses.

Ease the pain by rubbing with an onion.

Bathe with an infusion of hyssop leaves.

Burns
Honey applied to burns will help the pain and prevent blisters from forming.

Soak a soft cloth in cod-liver oil and place it on the burn.

Mix corn meal with powdered charcoal and add milk to make a paste for the burn.

Tie a piece of suet over the burn for quick healing.

Apply apple cider vinegar to affected area to remove soreness.

The pain of sunburn is eased by bathing frequently with cider vinegar.

Colds
When a cold is coming on, put blackberry cordial in a mug and top up with hot water. Drink the cordial in bed and go to sleep.

Drink hot milk with crushed garlic in it.

Spread goose grease on brown paper and put it on your chest.

Eat a hot roasted onion before going to bed to cure a cold.

Catnip and pennyroyal teas are both good for a cold.

Soak feet in hot water to get rid of a cold.

To clear head congestion, boil vinegar and water in a pot. Remove it from the heat and place your head, covered with a cloth, over the pot and inhale.

Drink whiskey heated with sugar and lemon, before going to bed.

Feed a cold and starve a fever.

Put your hat on the bedpost, get in bed and drink whiskey until you see two hats.

Corns
Bind on bread soaked in vinegar to remove corns. Reapply mornings and evenings.

Burn willow bark, and then mix the ashes with vinegar and apply to the corn.

Insert the toe in a lemon. Keep it on during the night. The corn can then be easily removed.

Corns should be treated with roasted onions mashed together and used as a poultice.

Soak feet in hot soapy water with vinegar to soften the corn.

Bind ivy leaves and vinegar onto the corn with a cloth.

Rub every day with a cut clove of garlic.

Cut corns in the waning moon and they will gradually disappear.

In 1902, Sears, Roebuck sold this 55¢ cure for corns and bunions. Early commercially made shoes sold to rural people were often limited in sizes and fit. The ball end of this tool was placed inside the shoe, leaving the ring outside. The handles were gently closed, stretching the leather over the painful spot without distorting the rest of the shoe.

Coughs
Slice an onion very thin, and alternate layers of onion and sugar. Place a plate on top to weigh them down. The juice that forms is soothing for a cough and safe for children.

Chop two large turnip roots into small pieces, and boil in a quart of water. Cool and strain. Add an amount of honey equal to whatever portion is taken.

Take a spoonful of kerosene mixed with sugar.

Cramps
Cramps in the neck or legs can be relieved by an application of whiskey and red pepper.

Drink warm pennyroyal tea.

Tie periwinkle stems around the leg or arm that is likely to be affected.

Cuts and Wounds
Remove the inside skin, or coating, from the shell of an uncooked egg. Place its moist side on a cut to promote healing.

Bathe the cut in a solution of water and baking soda. Sprinkle it, while still wet, with black pepper.

Cover a large cut with cow dung which is soft and creates heat. The cut will heal quickly.

Apply cobwebs to stop cuts from bleeding.

Press yarrow leaves to a cut to stop the flow of blood.

Bathe cuts with an infusion of marigold leaves to ease pain and lessen scarring.

Sprinkle the dried, powdered leaves of wild sunflowers on the wound to arrest blood flow.

Use a moist wad of chewing tobacco as a poultice.

Bruise peach tree leaves and put on the wound. Repeat as needed.

Diarrhea
In the summer, eat fresh blackberries, or boil blackberries in water, strain and drink the liquid.

Stew up garden rhubarb with some sugar, and eat a spoonful as long as necessary.

A tablespoonful of W.I. rum, a tablespoonful of molasses, and the same quantity of olive oil, well simmered together is helpful for this disorder.

Flour boiled thoroughly in milk, so as to make quite a thick porridge is good.

Flannel wet with brandy, powdered with cayenne pepper, and laid upon the bowels affords great relief in extreme distress.

Earache
To alleviate the slight earache, blow pipe or cigarette smoke into the ear.

To cure an earache, insert a piece of hot onion into the ear.

Put a few drops of hot sweet oil (olive oil) into the ear and plug with cotton.

Eyes
Black eyes can be eased by using a grated apple poultice.

Sore eyes can be treated with an eye wash made of apple juice.

Soak bread in a little milk and tie over the eye, and leave over night to relieve inflammation.

To help soreness, apply fresh green plantain leaves to the eyelids.

Cure a sty by putting grated potatoes, covered by a cloth, on the eye.

Wash weeping eyes with chamomile tea at night and in the morning

Feet
For offensive odor, soak feet in water in which green bark of oak has been boiled.

For excessive perspiration, put bran or oatmeal into the socks.

To relieve itching feet, soak every day in cider vinegar.

Fever
Pound horseradish leaves into a pulp. Apply to the soles of the feet to draw out fever.

Break a fever by drinking hot ginger tea.

Put slices of raw potato on the forehead to draw out a fever.

Hair
To make hair thicker, massage the juice of watercress into the scalp.

To get rid of dandruff, massage vinegar into scalp several times a week.

Hay Fever
Steep rose petals in a cup of hot water. Strain and apply drops to the eyes during the day to relieve irritation.

Mix leaves and flowers of goldenrod and ragweed. Put one-half ounce of the herbs in two cups of boiling water and allow to steep for ten minutes. Drink a small glassful four times a day to cure hay fever.

Headaches
Drink chamomile tea to soothe the head.

Bathe the forehead with hot water in which mint or sage has been boiled.

Cure a headache by swallowing a spider web.

Soak a cloth in warm vinegar and apply to the forehead.

Poison ivy or oak.
Mix powdered lime with lard until you have a paste and spread on the rash.

Apply milk, heavily salted, to skin affected by poison ivy. Allow to dry.

Slit the stem of jewelweed, and rub its sticky juice directly on the skin and let dry. When it starts to itch, reapply.

Squeeze the milk from the stems of milkweed and apply it to the rash.

Juice squeezed from the leaf of the elderberry and applied directly to the inflamed area will relieve the itch. Continue until the rash is gone.

Rheumatism and Arthritis
Keep rheumatism away by carrying a potato in the pocket, unseen by the opposite sex. The smaller and harder it becomes, the less likely the suffering from rheumatism.

Rub the aching limb with oil of mustard.

Take a teaspoon of cider vinegar every morning before breakfast.

Drink an infusion of marigold flowers four times a day.

Mix two teaspoons of cider vinegar and two teaspoons of honey into one-half cup warm water and drink three times a day.

Sore Throat
Gargle with warm, salt water.

Drink hot sage tea

Gargle with warm tea made from slippery elm bark.

Sugar and brandy relieves a sore throat.

A stocking bound on warm from the foot, at night, is good for the sore throat.

Stings and bites
Rub the spot with mashed plantain leaves.

Dab bee stings with household ammonia.

Rub dock leaf on insect stings, and also on nettle stings.

Apply mud to insect bites to relieve pain.

Dab stings with vinegar.

A slice of onion applied to an insect sting will take the pain away.

Rub vinegar or lemon juice on insect bites to eliminate the itch.

Stomach
Eat fresh mint or drink mint tea to settle an upset stomach.

Drink chamomile tea for an upset stomach.

Place crushed horseradish leaves directly on the skin over the stomach for aching.

Chop a clove of garlic and cover with a cup of boiling water. Drink when cool for indigestion.

Tea made from sheep droppings is good for stomach troubles.

Stop morning sickness by drinking a glass of water with a teaspoonful of vinegar upon rising.

A spoonful of ashes stirred in cider is good to prevent sickness at the stomach.

Teeth
To relieve a toothache, chew the leaves of catnip.

Treat toothache by putting a clove in the tooth, or using clove oil.

Whiten teeth by rubbing with powdered charcoal.

Prevent toothache by carrying a rabbit's tooth.

Warts
To remove warts, rub them with green walnuts.

Apply crushed marigold leaves and their juices to warts.

If horsehair is wrapped tightly around a wart, it will drop off.

Rub a snail on a wart to make it disappear.

Rub the wart with the furry inside of a broad bean pod.

The Weather

Weather Wisdom

When I was a child, I used to cross from one side of an estuary in Essex to a small island called Mersea. Our ferryman and his boat worked the oyster beds in the odd hours. Reuben was small and tough, with a weathered old face. He wore aged canvas pants, an old blue jersey, and boots that were folded above his knees. He did not have many teeth, and was the first man I'd ever seen with an earring. As we cast off with six passengers, it was clear, windy, and cold—typical for late May. Someone who had to return later asked about getting a trip back, because of the tide changes. Reuben looked up at the sky and said, "No later than three," because bad weather was on its way. We all looked at the white clouds scurrying along up in the blue and tried to guess what he meant. "I heard it on the weather forecast," he said.

For thousands of years, humans have devoted time and energy to the science of weather. Long before our sophisticated computer era, we watched the movements of the planets and the earth, we noted the directions of the winds and their effects, and we studied the actions and reactions of animals, insects, and plants. Today we recognize that the old ways—many with a saying or rhyme to carry the information—are sometimes as reliable as our modern methods.

For example, birds, animals, and insects are especially sensitive to changes in air pressure, and will alter their behavior before a storm. Cows tend to stay huddled together near the pasture gate if the weather is threatening, but they stroll around the pasture if it is going to be fine. They lie on the ground when it is going to rain, supposedly to keep themselves a dry spot on the grass. Frogs have a tendency to increase their serenading several hours before an incoming storm because the increased humidity keeps their skin moist and allows them to stay out of the water longer. And bees stick close to the hive before a storm.

Tornadoes

Tornadoes are extremely violent storms with intense winds in their vortex, which occur where cold and warm fronts collide. Updrafts in the center of the typical funnel cloud, which have been recorded at hundreds of miles per hour, can draw anything into the air and drop it some distance away. Once on the ground, tornadoes produce a terrifying roar. If your house is located in the central U.S., which has more tornadoes than anywhere else, or in any area known to have tornado activity, consult with your local authorities and prepare ahead of time. Watch thunder clouds for signs of a funnel, and have a plan of action for everyone in the family to follow. Many television and radio stations now have instant reporting systems that can track a tornado and give warning. Keep a portable radio with working batteries handy, as transmission wires are likely to be severed. If you have no "cyclone cellar," but do have a basement, position yourself in the southwest corner. Since tornadoes generally come from the southwest, if your house is hit, pieces are more likely to fall towards the northeast.

Lightning

We are all used to the thunder and lightning that occur throughout the country, generally on hot and humid afternoons and evenings. Lightning is a discharge of electricity that usually follows the easiest way to the ground. The high voltage can burn trees, damage buildings, cause combustible material to ignite, and kill people and animals. If you are indoors and see a storm approaching, unplug key electrical items such as computers and telephones, since lightning may enter the house through power or telephone lines. Stay away from open doors or windows. If you are outdoors, avoid any high place and get into a building. If there is no immediate shelter, look for a ditch or low spot to lie in or crouch down in the middle of a clump of trees. Do not get near or under a single tree since this is like being next to a lightning rod. Metal items, from backpacks to tractors, can also be dangerous in an electrical storm.

Altocumulus are mid-altitude clouds consisting of a layer of small cloudlets. They usually predict thunderstorms or rain within twenty-four hours.

Altostratus are mid-altitude clouds that block the light of the sun but are high enough to cast no shadows. Striated and dark gray in color, a darkening of this cloud cover indicates precipitation.

Cirrocumulus are high-altitude clouds that consist of a thin layer of ice crystals broken into bands or rows of small tufts by rising currents of air. They indicate unstable air and may lead to immediate precipitation.

Cirrocumulus undulatus are sheets of cirrocumulus with waves or undulations produced by the wind.

Cirrostratus are high-altitude clouds that consist of ice crystals and are spread out over a large area. Halos are sometime seen around these clouds, indicating precipitation.

Cirrus clouds are delicate, wispy swirls formed by high-altitude winds. They are often called mares' tails.

Cold fronts are the start of an air mass that is replacing warm air. It usually moves faster than a warm front and often brings brief, heavy rain.

Cumulonimbus are very large, thick clouds formed by strong thermals of moist, rising air that often reach a height of twelve miles where the jet stream shears off their tops and gives them the shape of anvils. Cumulonimbus clouds produce heavy rain and thunderstorms.

Cumulus, also called fair-weather cumulus, are small, white clouds with rounded tops and flattened bottoms. They form when the air is being warmed by the earth.

A typical anvil-shaped cumulonimbus cloud, which produces heavy rain and thunderstorms.

These cirrus clouds are commonly called mares' tails because their shape resembles the tail of a running horse. They sometimes precede a warm front that brings rain.

A lenticular cloud forms when moist air rises and condenses at the peak of a mountain. Since this condition only occurs at the peak, the cloud remains stationary.

Cumulus congestus clouds, darker on the bottom with peaks at the top, forming over the Florida Keys.

The sun hits drops of mist and is reflected back as a rainbow as this storm moves across Jackson Hole, Wyoming.

"Red sky at night, shepherd's delight. Red sky in morning, shepherds take warning." A red evening sky means the next day will be clear and calm, while red in the morning predicts rain before the day is out.

A dust devil is a small, spinning column of rising dust and air that occurs when the sun heats the ground. When it hits cooler ground, it loses its energy and disappears.

Frontal fog develops in advance of a warm front, when rain falling through cold air ahead of the front forms a mist near the ground.

Ground fog forms when the cold ground chills the air just above it. This fog is often seen early in the morning, before it is evaporated by the sun.

Hurricanes are tropical cyclones that form over warm ocean water. The wind must reach a speed of at least seventy-five miles an hour to qualify as a hurricane.

Nimbostratus, the largest of the low-altitude clouds, are thick and gray. They accompany a low-pressure front and produce heavy rain or snow.

Stratocumulus are low-altitude clouds seen when a stratus cloud breaks apart or when cumulus clouds come together at the same altitude.

Stratus are low-altitude, gray clouds that usually form when the earth's surface cools. Stratus clouds may result in drizzle or light snow.

A tornado is a violent and rapidly spinning vortex of air that has been generated in a thunderstorm.

Tropical storms are formed over the ocean and often develop into hurricanes as the winds accelerate their speed.

A warm front is the edge of a slow-moving air mass that is warmer than the one it is replacing. It is usually accompanied by precipitation.

Weather Lore

Whether the weather be cold,
Or whether the weather be hot,
We have to weather the weather
Whether we like it or not.

Red sky at night,
Shepherd's delight,
Red sky in the morning,
Shepherd's warning.

Dew in the night,
Next day will be bright

Grey mists at dawn,
The day will be warm

Rain before seven,
Fine before eleven.

A sun shiny shower,
Won't last half an hour

If the sun goes pale to bed,
'Twill rain tomorrow it is said.

Mackerel sky and mares' tails,
Make tall ships carry low sails.

Pale moon does rain,
Red moon does blow,
White moon does neither
rain nor snow.

When the stars begin to huddle,
The earth will soon become a puddle.

A rainbow at night,
Fair weather in sight.
A rainbow at morn,
Fair weather all gorn.

A foot deep of rain
Will kill hay and grain;
But three feet of snow,
Will make them grow mo'.

Who doffs his coat on a Winter's day,
Will gladly put it on in May.

Better to see a wolf in February
than a farmer in shirtsleeves

If February give much snow
A fine summer it doth foreshow.

Cows lying down in the pasture are harbingers of an approaching rainstorm.

Sheep leave higher elevations and head for low ground when weather threatens.

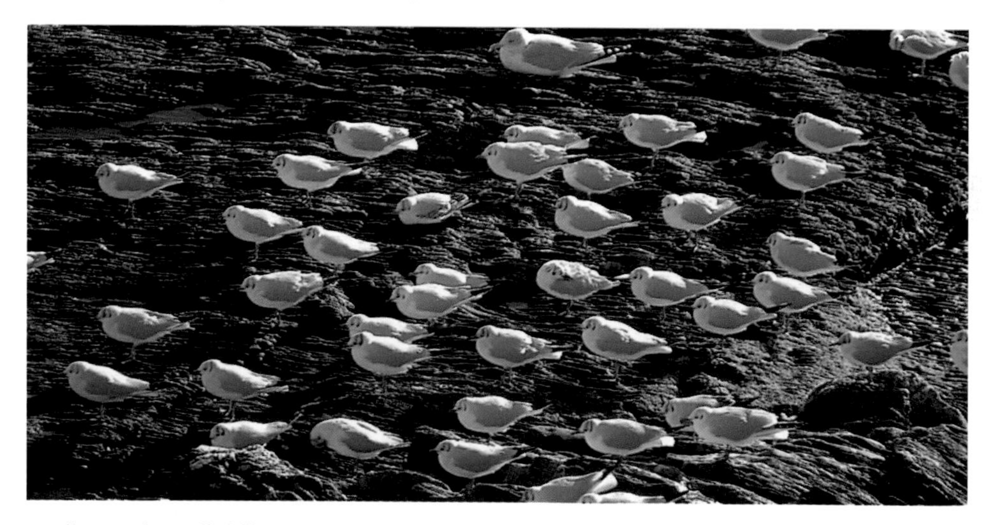

Gulls are often called "living weather vanes." They face into the wind so not to ruffle their feathers.

The rising sun colors these billowy cumulus, or fair-weather, clouds.

This tree attracted lightning that ran straight down the trunk to the ground. It's a clear example of why it makes sense to stay away from a tall tree during a thunderstorm.

If March comes in like a lion,
It goes out like a lamb.
If it comes in like a lamb,
It goes out like a lion.

A dry May and dripping June,
Brings everything in tune.

Dry August and warm
Doth harvest no harm.

Seagull, seagull,
get on the sand,
It's never fine weather
when you're on the land.

When a cow tries to scratch its ear,
It means a shower is very near.
When it clumps its side with its tail,
Look out for thunder, lightning and hail.

When the bees crowd out of their hive,
The weather makes it good to be alive.
When the bees crowd into their hive again,
It is a sign of thunder and rain.

Killing black beetles brings rain.

Onions skin very thin,
Mild winter coming in;
Onions skin thick and tough,
Coming winter will be rough.

Many holly berries, cold winter.

North wind brings hail,
South wind brings rain,
East winds we bewail,
West winds blow amain,
North-east wind is too cold,
South-east wind, not too warm,
North-west wind is far too bold,
South-west wind doth no harm

When the glass falls low,
Prepare for a blow;
When it rises high,
Let all your kites fly.

The weather's always ill
When the wind's not still

When the wind's in the East,
It's neither fit for man nor beast.

Those that are weatherwise
Are rarely otherwise.

Country Barn Raisings

In the happy event that you hear of a traditional barn raising, go to it. There will be lots to see and learn, and lots to do as well. You will certainly be well fed, but most importantly, you'll see how strangers are able to work together, have good evidence of it before sunset and, at the same time, become friends.

American farm buildings were well designed before nails and two-by-fours became the rule. The frames of barns, stables, and houses were pegged together and the main timbers were numbered, making them easy to take down and move elsewhere on the farm. Today, it often means taking the timbers to a new location to rescue a building from decay and oblivion. That is what friends of mine do—they save and restore worthwhile farm buildings and give them a new life. Re-raising these wonderful structures today doesn't really require a crowd of willing helpers, happy to spend a day working outdoors; after all, a complete barn frame can be put up with a crane and a half-dozen workers. But, from experience, there is nothing like the satisfaction and fun of being part of a team raising a barn the old way.

Here is a look at some traditional barn raisings: the first passages are personal accounts of typical 19th-century raisings; the later excerpt describes a barn being put up in one day a few years ago on a friend's small farm.

19th Century Barn Raising

About 1845, Grandfather built the new barn. He hired men to prepare the frame. They hewed the big timbers until they were squared to the proper dimensions for the foundations, uprights and great beams to hold the roof. Then they were mortised at the end and the proper places to insert the cross pieces and braces. Lastly, the rafters and ridge-pole were cut and piled ready to be quickly used without confusion. Finally wooden pins were made to fasten the frame together.
From *Aroostook Pioneers* by Mary Elizabeth Rogers

When the hands arrived, the great beams and posts and joists and braces were carried to their place on the platform, and the first bent was put together and pinned by the oak pins that the boys brought. Then the pike poles were distributed, the men, fifteen or twenty of them, arranged in a line abreast of the bent; the boss carpenter steadied and guided the corner post and gave the word of command. 'Take holt, boys!' 'Now set her up!' 'He-o-he!' (heave all heave), 'he-o-he!' at the top of his voice, every man doing his best. Slowly the great timbers go up; louder grows the word of command, till the bent is up. Then it is plumbed and stay lathed, and another is put together and raised in the same way, till they are all up. Then comes the putting on of the great plates, timbers that run lengthwise of the building and match the sills below. Then, the putting up of the rafters.
From *In the Catskills* by John Burroughs

As soon as the floor was laid, Bill and I set up plank tables and benches and the women brought pots of beans, brown bread, big roasts of veal and pork, a dozen pies and pitchers of cider. When Millie called, 'Victuals is ready,' there were thirty-eight hungry men washed up and ready to eat. Everyone was laughing and joking, and Millie and Annie ran back and forth between the table and the kitchen, bringing more pitchers of cider, tea, hot johnnycake, and more pie.
From *The Fields of Home* by Ralph Moody

. . . there was a dance on the big barn floor. On that ninety foot long floor the dancers had room aplenty to bow, circle, gallop and swing. The musicians, never more than three for such occasions, sat in the empty hayloft and played until two o'clock in the morning .
From *A Vanished World* by Anne Gertrude Sneller

A Barn Raising at Brier-Patch

Months of preparation preceded this day. The small forebay barn to be raised was first constructed before the middle of the 19th century by a man named Chamberline on a slope of his farm in Sand Brook, New Jersey. . . Beginning in late spring, the barn was carefully taken apart and trucked to the new site . . .

After an appropriate location was plotted, a substantial foundation for the barn was laid up in block and fieldstone. Next the timbers were repaired; in some cases replacement pieces were fashioned. The old sill and floor joist system was reassembled and a floor was laid. Framing members were inventoried and stocked in readiness around the site. The time had arrived for the raising . . .

With the gin pole in place, the raisers began assembling the first bent on the barn floor. Many hands were required to align the tenons with their corresponding mortises before the joints were finally closed with the beetle. . . . Those who assembled the sturdy oak frame could not help but appreciate the craftsmen of an earlier generation, who had skillfully cut the joints . . .

The strategy for raising the bents combined hoisting by hand with lifting with the block and tackle. At the direction of the boss carpenter to 'Heave ho!' some participants pulled the rope while others lifted together. The bent stirred, and rose slowly off the barn floor . . .

The barn raising took on a rhythm as periods of frenzy and excitement were interspersed with pauses for the relaxed preparation of the next state. Dogs ran in the field, musicians played, and many participants sat and talked and watched until the next call to raise a bent. . . .

Tired but happy, the members of the crew climbed down and stepped back to admire what they had accomplished. Silhouetted against the sunset, the barn frame looked noble and grandly serene. There had been no injuries other than a few souvenir splinters, though there would be some satisfyingly sore muscles the next day. In keeping with barn-raising tradition, a festive dinner was served. As the autumn chill returned to the air, a bonfire made of scraps of wood that had accumulated on the site lit the faces of the newly initiated, latter-day barn raisers.
From *Barn* by Elric Endersby, Alexander Greenwood, and David Larkin

Harvest

Once ended thy harvest, let none be beguil'd,
please such as did help thee, man, woman, and child;
Thus doing, with alway, such help as they can,
thou winnest the praise of the labouring man.

From *Five Hundred Good Points of Husbandry* by Thomas Tusser

Before the invention of the combine harvester, many hands were needed to cut and stack wheat before it was threshed and stored in the granary. As at the end of a successful barn or house raising, there were always feelings of pride and relief after a task well done—and a mood of celebration. It was thirsty work, and there was need for a "frolic" (from the Dutch *vroolijk*). On the next fine day, everyone would make a contribution by supplying the food, but it was the host who supplied the drink. The men and boys arranged competitive games involving feats of strength, balance, consumption of ale, and gumming (each contestant, head framed by a horse collar, tried to make the ugliest face). The women had competitions in quilting and spinning, but everyone joined in the singing and dancing. At one harvest event, two young ladies "spun a race" to determine who could lay claim to an eligible farmer. "*They began at six in the morning and spun until six in the evening. Two old ladies carded for them, one for each. At six o'clock Nancy was thirty rounds ahead. Forever afterward the fair Sarah had to look elsewhere for her swain.*"

From *Sugar Creek* by John Mack Faragher

The Old World harvest thanksgiving took place at the end of summer. The Puritans later moved it so that it would compete with Christmas. This lectern was used to read the lesson in the village church during the festival service. The European tradition of decorating altars and naves with farmers' produce and later giving it to the needy of the parish continues to this day. The book is Evelyn's *Silva*, my favorite source of information on timber and fruit trees.

In England also, the highlight of the farming year was the harvest. The men who cut the broad swathes up and down the field kept a lively pace. The farmer, knowing morale had to be high, sent out ale to refresh the workers. And when the last wagonload arrived home, the farmer would greet the workers with an invitation to a harvest dinner.

"And what a feast it was! Such a bustling in the farmhouse kitchen for days beforehand; such boiling of hams and roasting of sirloins; such a stacking of plum puddings, made by the Christmas recipe; such a tapping of eighteen-gallon casks and baking of plum loaves would astonish those accustomed to the appetites of today . . ."

From *The Village in England* by Graham Nicholson and Jane Fawcett

Celebrations

Weddings

Blessed is the bride whom the sun shines on.

If you marry when the moon is getting fuller, you will prosper.

It is lucky to marry in a snowstorm.

If a bride wishes to be prosperous in her married life, she must wear something old, something new, something borrowed and something blue.

Wedding gowns:
Married in white,
you have chosen right;
Married in green,
ashamed to be seen;
Married in gray,
go far away;
Married in red,
wish yourself dead;
Married in blue,
love ever true;
Married in yellow,
ashamed of your fellow;
Married in black,
wish yourself back;
Married in pink,
of you he'll always think.

Wedding days:
Monday for health,
Tuesday for wealth,
Wednesday the best
day of all,
Thursday for losses,
Friday for crosses,
Saturday no day at all.

From the gathering of the harvest until the twelfth night after Christmas, there is an almost unbroken chain of get-togethers and celebrations. The communal relief that country folk experienced when they knew there was enough food to last them through the dark winter and beyond made harvest time the crown of the farming year. Even in the 20th century, sunburned workers stand among the golden stooks, joining in ceremonies they have always been part of, but hardly aware that such events have been going on since the days of ancient Egypt, Greece, and Rome. For example, before any celebratory feasts, harvesters treat the last uncut stalks with reverence, taking the best ears to fashion into idols, or corn dollies that were brought into the farmhouse and hung there for a year. It was considered bad luck to remove them until the next harvest, when they were taken outside and burned. Corn dollies also were made by haystack thatchers, who would set them on the top of completed stacks to show off the quality and quantity of their work.

In Christian times, depending on when the parish felt that all the grains, fruits, and vegetables were safely gathered in, the church held Sunday thanksgiving services. In Britain, where observance is close to the actual harvest, it is also a popular time for weddings. Here, a church is beautifully decked out with the season's abundance.

Scarecrows

The Shakers said they grew a little extra for the birds and rodents, but most food growers consider themselves to be at war with the wild creatures who eat their produce. Anyone who has worked hard plowing, fertilizing, planting, and watching over crops has a very unsentimental view of the opponent.

When fields were smaller, farmers had all sorts of devices and schemes to scare birds away. There were two main methods: the first was to use an effigy of some sort and the second was noise. A combination would be running out in the field and shouting. In fruit-growing areas, children with rattles were employed. Rural calm was shattered a few years ago by powerful electronic air horns used by some farmers. The public soon put a stop to them when they malfunctioned and went off at night like huge car alarms.

As for those lonely scarecrow figures in the garden or field, we never know quite what makes them effective—or not. Some, knocked together from plastic bags, pantyhose, and old buckets work brilliantly, while others, fully rigged and realistic, become perches and even nests. Anyway, they are lots of fun. My battleground is our raspberry patch. I have tried bird netting (they fly under) and a very realistic owl with staring eyes, just like those used on the roofs of baseball stadiums. When I see droppings on its head, I know I have more to do.
There is another side to the scarecrow story, one that is a link to ancient times, when it was also known as a mawkin (from mannikin), hodmadod, and jackalent.
A figure, often of straw, would be used to protect cattle, promote fertility, as a bogie to protect crops, and to scare more than birds. At the end of the season it would be offered in sacrifice to be consumed on the top of a bonfire, like Halloween effigies or the English Guy Fawkes figures in our own time.

Superstitions

For good luck, sweep something into the house with a new broom, before you sweep something out.

It is bad luck to take an old broom to a new house.

Never buy a broom in May, for it sweeps all luck away.

Its bad luck to turn a strange cat away from the door

It is bad luck to make a new opening in an old house.

Leave a house by the same door through which you entered, or you will be unlucky.

If you rock the cradle empty, then you shall have babies plenty.

If your apron falls from your waist a new baby is on the way.

A pregnant woman should only look on beautiful things so that her child should likewise be born well-favored.

Newborns should be given three gifts: an egg to ensure plenty; silver to bring wealth; and salt for protection against enchantment.

If a baby is put in the first April shower, it will always be healthy.

A baby should be carried upstairs before downstairs so that it will rise in the world.

To change a baby's name after you have named it will cause it to have bad luck all of its life.

Holly was hung on the door at Christmas so that witches would stay outside counting berries.

A horseshoe hung over the door, right way up to keep in the goodness, will keep witches away.

Horse brasses hung over the fireplace are also a protection against witches.

Wood spitting in the fireplace was believed to be the Devil coming down the chimney.

Sneezing at the table is a sign of company at the next meal.

If you sneeze while something is being said it is the truth

If you dream of a river, it means that something stands between you and your wishes.

To dream of snakes brings bad luck.

If you eat black-eyed peas on New Year's Day, you will have good luck all the year.

A man must be the first person to cross your threshold on New Year's Day, or you will have bad luck throughout the coming year.

When starting a journey, throw salt over your right shoulder to ensure safety.

If you catch a falling leaf, you will have twelve months of happiness.

To find a rusty nail is good luck. The nail should not be picked up, but the ends should be reversed, so luck will come your way.

Stems of tea floating in the cup indicate strangers. The time of their arrival is determined by placing the stem on the back of one hand and smacking it with the other; the number of blows given before it is removed indicate the number of days before the stranger's arrival.

It is unlucky to eat a fish from the head downwards; secure good luck by eating the fish from the tail towards the head.

If a married man dreams that he is being married, it means that he is going to die.

If you bring an axe or hoe or spade into the house on your shoulder, a member of the family will die soon.

If a person dreams that he sees a naked figure dancing in the air, it means that death will come and release a soul from its body.

If rain falls on a coffin, it indicates that the soul of the departed has "arrived safe."

Never carry a corpse to church by a new road.

If a cock crows at midnight, the angel of death is passing over the house.

The howling of a dog is a sad sign. If repeated for three nights, the house will soon be in mourning.

After a person dies, cover all the mirrors in the house to prevent the soul being caught.

Hag stones—flints with holes in them—were at one time thought to be a safeguard against witches or evil, and were hung on stables and barns and under eaves of houses, or even carried in the pocket. And, if tied to the head of the bed, they would prevent nightmares.

Rocks, of natural formation, with an opening or hole through which a person could crawl were thought to promote cures for backache, rheumatism and other ills.

Jump across the doorsill when entering the house at night, so the spook cannot get hold of the heel left behind the other.

Glastonbury Tor in the distance has more legends and superstitions connected to it than any other place in Britain.

Some Grave Humor

The common gravestone probably originated as a flat slab, an effort to protect the corpse from wild beasts. In the Western world, it rose up first as a form of identification and then as the background of an epitaph, a pious inscription giving an opinionated view of the life of the deceased. Quotations offered advice and warnings from the grave. Early country epitaphs minced no words and used no soft expressions to veil the facts: sinners were sinners and saints were saints. Skulls are on the earliest stones but, gradually, sentiment began to appear. First, the skull got wings to fly to heaven, next the head was fleshed out a bit, a wig was added and then curls, and so on until a chubby cherub symbolizing everlasting peace and hope adorned many gravestones. The words, also, were under the control of the survivors, who often looked at the face of death and told it like it was, using vernacular puns, jokes, and insults. In today's light, there is some unconscious humor, too, in spelling mistakes, and in my favorites, Victorian moral encouragements. Like good stories, some epitaphs travelled far and were borrowed throughout the English-speaking world within a surprisingly short time.

Thank you sweet battle axe for
23 years of hell and happiness.
DELAWARE

He recommended himself very
highly
DELAWARE

I told you I was sick.
DELAWARE

Here lies the body of Mrs.
Mary,
wife of Dea. John Buel ESQ.
She died Nov. 4 1768 Aged 90
Having had 13 children
101 grand-children
274 great-grand-children
49 great-great-grand children
410 Total. 336 survived her.
CONNECTICUT

Soon ripe
Soon rotten
Soon gone
But not forgotten.
MASSACHUSETTS

Hail!
This stone marks the spot
Where a notorious sot
Doth lie:
Whether at rest or not
It matters not to you or I.
ENGLAND

Sacred to the memory of
three twins.
VERMONT

Of children in all she
bore twenty-four
Thank the Lord
there will be no more.
ENGLAND

This is what I expected but
not so soon
(age 21)
NEW YORK

Fair Maiden Lilliard
lies under this stone
Little was her stature,
but great was her fame.
Upon the English lions
she had laid many thumps,
And when her legs was cutted off,
she fought upon her stumps.
SCOTLAND

Here lies one Wood enclosed in wood,
One Wood within another.
The outer wood is very good,
We cannot praise the other.
MAINE

Gone to be a angle.
TENNESSEE

Under this pile of stones
Lie the remains of Mary Jones.
Her name was Lloyd, it was not Jones,
But Jones was put to rhyme with stones.
AUSTRALIA

This rose was sweet a while,
But now is odour vile.
NEW HAMPSHIRE

Sacred to the memory of
Anthony Drake,
Who died for peace and quietness sake;
His wife was constantly
scolding and scoffin',
So he looked for repose
in a twelve-dollar coffin.
MASSACHUSETTS

This disease you ne'er heard tell on —
I died of eating too much melon;
Be careful, then, all you that feed—
I Suffered because I was too greedy.
ENGLAND

We can but mourn our loss,
Though wretched was his life.
Death took him from the cross,
Erected by his wife.
MAINE

Here lies the body of
Thomas Vernon
The only surviving son
of Admiral Vernon
ENGLAND

Stranger call this not a place
Of fear and gloom,
To me it is a pleasant spot
It is my husband's tomb.
MASSACHUSETTS

She lived with her husband
fifty years
And died in the confident
hope of a better life.
VERMONT

Grieve not for me, my husband dear,
I am not dead, but sleepest here,
With patience wait, prepare to die,
And in a short time you'll come to I.
(added later)
I am not grieved my dearest life;
Sleep on, I have another wife;
Therefore, I cannot come to thee,
For I must go and live with she.
ENGLAND

My wife lies here.
All my tears cannot bring her back;
Therefore, I weep.
VERMONT

Halloween

Interest in Halloween is much stronger in the United States than in Europe, where it originated. An Irish import that seems to grow more popular here each year, it bridges the original harvest season and Thanksgiving. I love it, but my Irish forbears in Britain paid it little attention, and I don't remember being aware of Halloween during the two autumns I spent in Ireland. The timing is right, with that first real chill in the air and the leaves colored like flames. The clocks are just back an hour, so dusk arrives earlier. It seems a good occasion for something to happen.

The Celts thought of this time as the end of the old year. The spirits and souls of the dead would arise for one night before they could begin a new year. In Christian times, this night became All Hallows Eve, Hallowmass, or Night of the Dead. It was a time to pray against evil and tell stories about ghosts. Country folk would scare off these ghosts by pretending to be spirits themselves and lighting big bonfires for courage. The lads would get up to mischief, riding farmers' horses around at night to make them sweat as if they had been ridden by fairies, or stealing and putting the blame on witches. They also used the occasion to settle old scores, perhaps those originating at the other end of the year, May Day, when their romancing had been stopped by the father of a love interest.

Jack O'Lantern was an Irish ghost who carried glowing embers from hell in a large turnip hollowed out to make a lamp for his journey back to earth. Where we live, the bigger pumpkin makes a brighter lantern.

This group was carved by Tennessee schoolchildren.

Yuletide

The darkest part of the year is a good time to have a party. Before Christianity, people in the northern hemisphere knew that the winter solstice occurred when the night was longest, with the sun slowly returning to bring more light each day. With that in mind, exactly halfway through their winter gloom was a time for feasting. Ancient Romans celebrated Saturnus, the god of agriculture. Slaves were temporarily free, presents were exchanged, candles were lit, and evergreens were brought in to decorate the halls. The carnival, which means "finishing off" the meat, went on for days. Most scholars agree that Christians, for their own purposes, appropriated celebrations that had been going on for centuries. Beginning in medieval times, grain, nuts, fruit, and root crops from the harvest were carefully stored, and geese and swine were fattened for the winter feast.

Now the feasting, for the most part, begins on Christmas Eve and continues Christmas Day, and it evokes the traditions of all the people who settled America.
As immigrant groups were folded into American culture, they gradually centered their celebrations around Christmas rather than St. Nicholas' Day, St. Lucia's Day, or Three Kings' Day, for example. However, each group prepared the symbolic and festive foods that had been traditional for centuries, often as far back as pagan times. Many of these delights take the form of sweets ranging from yeast breads, cakes, and pies to cookies, fritters, and puddings. Around Christmas, depending on where you live, you might be able to sample Mexican *buñuelos,* Italian *panettone,* German *stollen,* Swedish gingersnaps, English plum pudding with lucky coins, Puerto Rican *arroz con dulce,* or special breads from Czechoslovakia, Austria, Sweden, Finland, Greece, and most other European countries.

In America, because of the structure of communities, Christmas dinner seems to have no fixed time.
In Germany it takes place at four o'clock on Christmas Eve, in France after midnight when the meal is ended with a chocolate Yule log, or *Bûche de Noël.* The British have their dinner in the early afternoon on Christmas Day, and get ready for parties with more food in the evening. The feast itself hardly ever changes. It has always been loaded with special treats, with hosts eager to show the amount of the harvest used for the celebration.

As Stephen Nissenbaum pointed out in his excellent book, *The Battle for Christmas,* all the trappings for the holiday were in place before the church got control—the bringing in of holly, ivy, laurel, mistletoe, and pine boughs to festoon the halls; the huge Yule log burning for days, a symbol that kept the merrymaking going until it turned to ashes; home-brewed wine and beer to be consumed with the precious roasted meat. This was the only time of the year that folk in the country, who had grown this feast, had anything really good to eat. Today, when most of us have plenty throughout the year, we have to think about how rare this occasion was—and still is—for all too many of us. The early colonists saw it as a time of indulgence, which they wished to avoid. They came to the New World to get away from excess, sure that Hugh Latimer, a 16th-century Anglican bishop, was right in saying: "Men dishonor Christ more in the twelve days of Christmas, than in all the twelve months besides."

The early part of the 17th century was an active time for the Puritans in England and the New World, who resolutely obtained religious and political control over their fellow citizens. The Puritan fathers were aware of the pagan connections to Christmas, and did not want the plain Christian holy days usurped by men and women who, in their opinion, just wanted to have a good time.
So, in 1659, the Massachusetts Bay Colony outlawed Christmas as a public holiday. Anyone could be fined for feasting, drinking, or not working. The law was never totally successful, although it was nearly one hundred years before Christmas as a joyous festival recovered in New England.

Mince pies being prepared just before Christmas.

In the meantime, each ethnic group brought Christmas traditions to these shores, and today we have a happy mixture. For example, the Christmas tree, an old symbol of growth and light, was rediscovered in parts of Germany in the 18th century and established in Britain and America in the early 1800s. The singing of carols out-of-doors in the village square or at the front door follows from an ancient excuse to go wassailing (from the Anglo Saxon *Wes ha'l,* meaning "good health"). As many English children did, I knew a lot of carols and their verses. We would get a good number of carolers together to sing, like medieval wassailers, outside a house until someone opened the door and paid us to go away. The tradition of giving on Christmas Eve goes back to the Old Country: to Sweden where sheaves of grain were left outside for the birds, France where bread was given to the stable animals, Poland where porridge was put out to keep Jack Frost away from the young crops, and Denmark where rice pudding, with a pink pig in it, was put in the attic for the elves. We can see how Santa Claus got his milk and cookies.

Another symbol—St. Nicholas, Kriss Kringle, Santa Claus, or Father Christmas—is still evolving. For this season, his invention as a distributor of gifts and an arbiter of good behavior in the young is convenient and worth preserving. Where did he come from? He is an icon with a costume different in each country where he is known. For example, in Holland, as St. Nicholas, he has a long gown, originates from the 4th century, and visits on December 6. All that is common today is the beard and the red clothing, a connection to his past as a bishop.

MAGDAL
VINERY
LIMITED
QUALITY
WINES

Conclusion

E.M. Forster's novel *Howards End* has passages evoking the pleasure of retreating to a charming old house in the bluebell forest. When the royalties from his books began to pile up, Forster acquired such a place, complete with its own woods. Then the gentle, ecologically minded democrat became a narrow-minded conservative when he said, "It was intersected, blast it, by a public footpath." He wanted solitude and the exclusive freedom of the surroundings. Strangers, whether humans, deer, or squirrels, would be after *his* flowers, fruits, and nuts. He didn't much like the idea, either, that his favorite birds might fly off to a more attractive or rewarding location.

Having a place in the country, it is sometimes difficult to overcome the territorial imperative buried in all of us. It has taken me some years to stop worrying about hunters' guns, or chain saw, snowmobile, and heavy equipment noises sounding nearer than they should. Rarely is there something amiss; we all do get along; and I personally feel encouraged that the countryside where I live is returning in large part to its natural state more quickly than we can destroy it. I keep discovering some new plant, or new use of a familiar one, and changes in natural conditions and habitats that further encourage my confidence and sense of security in living within the countryside. And perhaps even leaving it more naturally productive for all species doesn't seem now to be as difficult as I thought it would be when we first arrived and began to make a home.

Bibliography

Angier, Bradford. *Field Guide to Edible Wild Plants.* Harrisburg, Pennsylvania: Stackpole Books, 1974.

Belanger, Jerome D. *The Homesteader's Handbook to Raising Small Livestock.* Emmaus,Pennsylvania: Rodale Press Inc., 1974.

Buchanan, Rita. *A Dyer's Garden.* Loveland, Colorado: Interweave Press, 1995.

Child, Mrs. *The American Frugal Housewife.* Boston: Carter, Hendee, and Co., 1833.

Erichsen-Brown, Charlotte. *Medicinal and Other Uses of North American Plants.* New York: Dover Publications, 1989.

Endersby, Elric, Alexander Greenwood, and David Larkin. *Barn: The Art of a Working Building.* Boston: Houghton, Mifflin Company, 1992.

Evans, George Ewart. *Ask the Fellows Who Cut the Hay.* London: Faber and Faber, 1961.

Faragher, John Mack. *Sugar Creek: Life on the Illinois Prairie.* New Haven: Yale University Press, 1986.

Foster, Steven, and James A. Duke. *A Field Guide to Medicinal Plants.* Boston: Houghton Mifflin Company, 1990

Garrett, Wendell. *American Colonial.* New York: The Monacelli Press, 1994.

Halstead, Byron D., ed. *Barns, Sheds and Outbuildings.* Lexington , Massachusetts: The Stephen Greene Press, 1977.

Harman, Tony. *Seventy Summers: The Story of a Farm.* London: BBC Books, 1986.

Hartley, Dorothy. *Lost Country Life.* London: Macdonald & Janes Publishers, Ltd., 1979.

Lincoff, Gary H. *The Audubon Society Field Guide to North American Mushsrooms.* New York: Knopf, 1981.

Martin, George A. *Fences, Gates and Bridges.* New York: O. Judd Co., 1887.

Moody, Ralph. *The Fields of Home.* New York: Norton, 1953.

Nissenbaum, Stephen. *The Battle for Christmas.* New York: Alfred A. Knopf, 1996.

Noble, Allen G. *To Build in a New Land: Ethnic Landscapes in North America.* Baltimore: The Johns Hopkins Press, 1992.

___________. *Wood, Brick and Stone: Barns and Farm Structures.* Amherst: The University of Massachusetts Press, 1984.

Peterson, Lee. *A Field, Guide to Edible Wild Plants of Eastern and Central North America.* Boston: Houghton Mifflin, 1978.

Phillips, C. E. Lucas. *The Small Garden.* London: Pan Books Ltd., 1956.

Phillips, Roger. *Mushrooms of North America.* Boston: Little, Brown and Company, 1991.

___________. *Wild Food.* Boston: Little Brown and Company, 1983.

Phillips, Roger, and Nicky Foy. *Herbs.* London: Pan Books Ltd., 1990.

Phillips, Roger, and Martyn Rix. *Vegetables.* London: Pan Books Ltd., 1993.

Pollan, Michael. *Second Nature: A Gardener's Education.* New York: Atlantic Monthly Press, 1991.

Sneller, Anne Gertrude. *A Vanished World.* Syracuse: Syracuse University Press, 1964.

Williams, Henry L. and Ottalie K. Willliams. *How to Furnish Old American Houses.* New York: Farrar, Straus & Giroux, Inc., 1949.

Acknowledgments

I would like to thank the following for their help in the preparation of this book:

Chris and Edna Bergstrom; Lois Brown; Bill Byrne; Tommy Candler and Alan Plaistowe; Canterbury Shaker Village; Russell A. Cohen; Steve Davis; Ronnie and Becky Dodd; Lorin Driggs; Dorothy Elliott; Elric Endersby and Alexander Greenwood; Edie Evans; Denis Farina; Liza Fosburgh; Nicky Foy; Michael and Neyla Freeman; A. Blake Gardner; Doris Halle; John and Betty Holmes; Marc and Vivienne Jaffe; Ian Ross Jenkins and Maria Carvainis; James Kunkle; Anna Larkin; Colin Larkin; Ellen Larkin; Kay Larkin; Sally Larkin; Terry McAweeney; Arthur Magri; Roger Phillips; Robert H. Robinson; Paul and Elaine Rocheleau; Brian and Lizzie Sanders; Meg Schaefer; Judith Storie; Anita Carroll-Weldon; the Zema Family. The decoration above the title on page 2 is an overmantel cresting in linden, carved by David Esterly in 1994 (photo: Ildiko Butler).

Photo Credits

The Barn People: 117 bottom left.

Bill Byrne: 19, 28, 30 bottom, 34, 35, 36, 67.

Tommy Candler: 2, 6, 47, 48, 89, 93 bottom right, 95, 96 top, 100 left, 128-129, 134, 138, 139, 140, 142 top, 143, 144 top and bottom, 145, 146, 151, 153, 162, 163, 168 top, 188, 191 left and right, 195 top left, 197 top, 225 top, 237, 250 left and right, 251 bottom left, 277 bottom, 279 top, 286, 287, 291, 296, 298, 302.

Bruce Coleman Inc.: Adrian Davies 279 bottom; Keith Gunnar 279 top; Dotte Larsen 276 bottom; C.C. Lockwood 290 left; S. Nielsen 276 center; Masha Nordbye 276 top; Mike Price 277 top and bottom; Bradley Simmons 274; Steve Solum 289; Gary Witney 273; Jonathan Wright 104, 105, 130-31.

Steve Davis, Living History Farms: 141.

Michael Freeman: 49 top, 120, 121, 125 bottom, 126, 135, 181 top and bottom right, 198-199, 204-05, 211 top and bottom right, 214. 216-17, 217 bottom right, 218, 219, 240-41, 242, 246-47, 247 right, 248, 251 top right, 256, 257, 260, 262, 266, 290-91, 293.

A. Blake Gardner: 10, 11, 12 top, 18, 21, 22, 23, 25, 26-27, 29, 30 top, 31 top, 32, 33, 37, 38, 40-41, 43, 44, 45, 50-51, 58, 64, 74, 99 left and right.

Robert Harding Picture Library: 278 top, center and bottom; 299.

Fred Hoogervorst: 108. 112, 113.

Chuck Kidd: 281.

David Larkin: 9, 16 bottom, 13, 14, 15, 24, 39, 49 bottom, 56 bottom, 57 bottom, 59, 60, 61, 62, 66, 69, 70, 71, 81, 82, 83 top, 90 top, 91 left, 100 right, 102, 106, 109, 114 right, 115 top left, 115 bottom left and right, 116 left, 117 top, 122, 127, 132, 133, 136, 142 bottom, 152, 155, 157, 159, 161, 165, 168 bottom, 169 top, 170 bottom, 171 bottom, 172 left, 174, 175, 181 left and middle right, 183 top, 192 top, 196, 197 bottom, 202, 208 top, 210, 213 bottom right, 225 bottom right, 263, 264 right, 265 top, bottom right and left, 285, 290 right, 292, 294 top, 295.

The New Jersey Barn Company: 114 left, 115 top right, 117 bottom right.

Roger Phillips: 16, 17, 53, 54, 55, 56 top, 57 top, 65, 72, 73, 76, 77, 78, 79, 83 bottom, 84, 85, 86, 97, 88, 90 bottom, 91 right, 92-93 top, 93 bottom left, 94, 96 bottom, 97, 98, 100 right, 101 left, 154, 156, 158, 160, 164, 166, 167, 169 bottom, 170 top, 172 right, 173, 176, 177, 178-79, 180, 182, 183 bottom, 184-85, 186-87, 189, 192 bottom, 193, 194, 195 top right and bottom left and right.

Paul Rocheleau: 8, 20, 107, 116, 118, 119, 123, 124, 125 top, 137, 148-49, 190, 201, 203, 206, 207, 208 bottom, 212-13, 220-21, 221 bottom right, 222, 223, 224, 228-29, 230-31, 232, 233, 234-25, 236, 238-39, 244, 245, 249, 252, 253, 255, 258-59, 264 left, 268-69, 270, 280, 282, 283, 284, 288.

Elizabeth Whiting Associates: 297.